GREATEST GAMES
MANCHESTER CITY

GREATEST GAMES
MANCHESTER CITY

DAVID CLAYTON

First published by Pitch Publishing, 2013

Pitch Publishing

A2 Yeoman Gate

Yeoman Way

Durrington

BN13 3QZ

www.pitchpublishing.co.uk

ISBN 978-1-9091787-1-7

Typesetting and origination by Pitch Publishing

Printed and bound by CPI Group (UK) Ltd, Croydon, CR0 4YY

Contents

Dedication

For Jeff, Gill, Ally and Joe. Welcome home.

Acknowledgements

THANKS TO Paul Camillin at Pitch Publishing for all his support and, as per usual, his patience – plus the editing team at Pitch. Thanks to my family and to all the City fans who helped along the way with memories of games and moments that made each match special. Thanks to Chris and Vicky, too.

A special thanks to Tony Brown of the excellent stats site The English National Football Archive (www.enfa.co.uk).

Introduction

GREATEST GAMES aren't always cup finals and title deciders, which, as a lifelong Blue, is just as well as I would have been struggling to fill this book! City, of course, haven't always been able to send out a starting XI full of stellar names and familiar faces and over the past 40 years or so there have been plenty of journeymen and bargain buys who've donned the sky blue jersey. For 35 years, we didn't even have a trophy to show for the 1,500 or so matches played during that period.

But as any Blue will tell you, there has been plenty of drama and many unforgettable games. It is not all about Champions League Finals and Premier League and FA Cup doubles, even though we wouldn't say no.

Our memories as City fans are filled with just as much drama and rollercoaster moments – our club more than most – and that's what I've tried to capture in this book.

While most of the games you would expect to find in a collection such as this are indeed here, there are a few curveballs that might evoke some raised eyebrows and a couple that might even raise the question, 'Why?'

Well, there's a reason behind each one and while some may be more obvious than others, I hope you enjoy reading about one or two gems that might have otherwise been forgotten and confined to a stat in a history book.

I reckon the next few years will probably yield another 20 or so new matches that could live happily in this book so with that in mind, here's to the revised edition in 2015!

Until then, here are 60 that should certainly stick in the memory banks for one reason or another.

Enjoy the book and thanks for reading it. I'll see you at the Etihad.

David Clayton, Manchester, 2013

v QPR 3-2

13 May 2012
Premier League
Attendance: 47,435

MANCHESTER CITY:	QUEENS PARK RANGERS:
Hart	Kenny
Zabaleta	Hill
Clichy	Taiwo
Kompany	Ferdinand
Lescott	Onuoha
Barry (Dzeko 69)	Derry
Yaya Toure (De Jong 45)	Barton
Silva	Wright-Phillips
Nasri	Mackie
Aguero	Cisse (Traore 59)
Tevez (Balotelli 74)	Zamora (Bothroyd 76)

WHEN WE'RE talking about greatest games, there's really only one place to start, isn't there? This isn't just one of City's best ever matches, it's one of the most incredible games of football there has ever been with more twists and turns than an Agatha Christie novel and an ending that was pure Hollywood make-believe.

City had somehow clawed their way back into the title race having seemingly been left for dead by Manchester United on the run-in and with just six games to go, the Blues had fallen eight points adrift of the leaders.

United's spectacular implosion in the games that remained meant City knew they needed only to win the final match of the campaign to complete a remarkable turnaround in fortunes and lift the Premier League title for the first time – simple!

Well, at least it looked that way on paper.

After a season that had so many twists and turns, the events of this match should have been no real surprise to those gathered in the Etihad Stadium or the millions watching and listening around the world.

This was drama, excitement and fate all combined in one explosive game that is perhaps one of the greatest games of football ever seen. The stars aligned to produce a gamut of raw emotions and a rollercoaster of despair and ecstasy in equal measure.

So where to begin? QPR, managed by former City boss Mark Hughes, were the opposition and they also had plenty riding on this result.

A defeat for the Hoops and a win for Bolton at Stoke and they would be condemned to an immediate return to the Championship. They had to give their all and despite possessing an awful away record, they had to believe they could spoil the party.

Apart from the manager being an ex-Blue, they also had three players who had all been popular during their time with City in the shape of Joey Barton, Shaun Wright-Phillips and Nedum Onuoha who would, on another day, have all been willing their former club to win the title.

But not today. There was tension in the air as the teams came out, but there was also expectancy. Roberto Mancini's side had been sweeping opposition away all season – particularly at home – and the way the Blues had kept their belief when all seemed lost made a win seem like the obvious end to the fairytale.

The fans were geared up for a party and no matter how many times the club had shot itself in the foot at the most inopportune moments, this team of winners would see the job through and bring the title home. At least, that's how it seemed.

The early indications were the game would go to form as QPR defended with ten men behind the ball in an effort to snuff out City's creativity, particularly around the edge of the box.

Sheer weight of numbers meant the first half-hour was frustrating to say the least as Rangers defended for their lives and when the defensive block was penetrated, Paddy Kenny in the QPR goal was in inspired form, blocking, clawing and scrambling clear whatever came his way.

Just as it seemed the Blues would have to settle for a goalless first half, the breakthrough – at last – came. Pablo Zabaleta's shot wasn't the cleanest hit he'll make in his career but Kenny's efforts to save it saw the ball loop up and hit the far post before nestling in the back of the net to put City 1-0 up.

Surely now everyone could sit back and relax? QPR had other ideas and the second half was barely three minutes old when the visitors, abandoning their parking of the bus tactics, came out as though they had been released of their shackles and suddenly looked a different proposition.

When Wright-Phillips lofted a ball through the middle, Joleon Lescott was flat-footed as he attempted to head it clear and merely directed it into the path of Djibril Cisse who raced through and lashed a powerful shot past Joe Hart to make it 1-1.

The doubts that had bubbled beneath the surface emerged again and the game took on another dimension. QPR, fairly resolute at the back, could sniff blood and the apprehension and anxieties of the City fans filtered down to the pitch where mistakes were now being made.

Yet the equilibrium again seemed to tilt the Blues' way as Carlos Tevez and Barton clashed on the edge of the QPR box on 55 minutes.

It was hard to make out what had happened at first but the assistant referee on the far side had seen enough and flagged for Mike Dean's attention. Barton had elbowed Tevez in the face as the pair challenged for a loose ball and the ex-City man had been spotted and was shown a straight red card as a result. Barton hung around long enough to irreparably damage his career in England as he squared up to whoever challenged him and then gave Sergio Aguero a punch in the ribs as he departed. It was chaos.

The incident seemed to rattle City more than ten-man QPR and within ten minutes, the Hoops were ahead as Traore skipped past Vincent Kompany before teeing up a superb cross for Jamie Mackie who arrived just in time to send a downward header past Hart and send the 3,000 travelling fans wild.

The Etihad Stadium was in shock, the City players were stunned and there was utter disbelief at the story unfolding before their eyes. With United winning at Sunderland, the prospect of blowing it at home to a team fighting relegation was becoming all too real.

There were still 23 minutes left, but by now, the vast majority had convinced themselves that there was no way back and the 'Typical City' tag everyone hoped had been banished forever was about to have one last torturous laugh.

City threw on Edin Dzeko and Mario Balotelli and QPR reverted to type, defending as a unit in and around their box as they played out the final minutes of what looked like being the ultimate smash-and-grab.

The Blues continued to create chances but a mixture of poor finishing, brave defending and the inspirational Kenny kept everything out.

The 90 minutes were up and the board went up for five additional minutes as City, running out of gas and ideas, won their 19th corner of the afternoon. Silva whipped the ball in and Dzeko leapt to head home from close range. It was 2-2 and there was still enough time for one more attack.

Many didn't celebrate the goal, feeling it was one more cruel twist of the knife. News was filtering through from other grounds – QPR were safe after Bolton failed to beat Stoke and suddenly the visiting fans were urging City to go forward and win the game. United had won at Sunderland so the Blues had to score again.

Zabaleta challenged Wright-Phillips near the halfway line and Samir Nasri allowed the ball to run out of play. QPR throw. Nasri thought it was City's and hung on to the ball for what seemed like an eternity, much to the chagrin of the crowd who just wanted the game to continue.

Onuoha took a long throw down the line and the ball was won back by City and played to Nigel de Jong who carried it into the QPR half. The Rangers players continued to retreat and allowed him to find Aguero who had found a pocket of space near the edge of the box.

He played to Balotelli who held off his marker and as he fell to the ground he nudged the ball back into Aguero's path. The Argentine beat one man then feigned to shoot and took out another before rifling a low shot past Kenny – cue pandemonium! City had conjured up two goals in injury time and were 3-2 up – it was incredible, exhilarating and unbelievable. Impossible even.

The Etihad Stadium went crazy – the QPR fans celebrated and a few moments later, the referee blew for full time and City were crowned Premier League champions.

For sheer theatre and drama, it's hard to imagine this game ever being beaten, yet fate had played its hand, too.

It felt like, while City's name had been on the trophy all along, the Blues' fans would have to be pushed to the absolute edge of the abyss before being allowed to celebrate.

City fans have come to expect nothing less and as the players collected their prize to a shower of fireworks and tickertape, people were still asking themselves, 'Did that really just happen?'

Mancini said afterwards, 'You would probably be talking to a different manager if we hadn't won that game. But I never think about this. I think we have a very good memory from last season.

'Football is beautiful for this reason, because anything can happen in one game. In the last game, we had 44 chances to score, QPR had three and they scored two goals.

'We had a problem with our heart but in the end it was good. But we didn't win the championship in the last few seconds of that game.

'We won the championship during all of the season because we deserved to win it and we did better than all the other teams.

'I never stopped believing, never. But, when there are three or four minutes to the end and you're 2-1 down, it's difficult.

'In the end we deserved it. That last game was crazy. It was impossible to think the game could finish like that.

'When you win a title like we did, one result can change the situation. But in two years we did a good job and worked well. We improved every year.

'Last season our target was to fight for the title until the last game and we did that. It's important for us to work well because we want to stay on the top for a long time.

'We want to stay there for ten or 15 years.'

The stats suggested the result was the right one – City had conjured up 35 shots to QPR's three – two of which ended with a goal and the corner count was City 19 QPR 0.

As Sky Sports commentator Martin Tyler correctly said, 'I swear you'll never see anything like this again. So watch it. Drink it in.'

And drink we did …

v **Newcastle United** 3-3

Premier League
24 February 1996
Attendance: 31,115

MANCHESTER CITY:	NEWCASTLE UNITED:
Immel	Srnicek
Summerbee	Barton
Hiley	Beresford
Curle	Albert
Symons	Peacock
Brown	Howey
Clough	Clark
Lomas	Ferdinand
Kinkladze	Beardsley
Quinn	Asprilla
Rosler	Ginola

KEVIN KEEGAN'S Newcastle United – dubbed 'The Entertainers' by the media – rolled in to Maine Road with most of the nation willing them to keep winning games in order to stay ahead of Manchester United in the race for the Premier League title.

At the time, it was a tough one for most Blues fans! In the build-up to the game, United supporters claimed that City would roll over to help the Geordies edge towards the championship trophy but, of course, this would be anything but the case, as ensuing events would prove.

In fact, history has shown that whenever the Reds need a favour from City, for some reason, the Blues always come through. You just can't count on anyone these days …

It was a crisp and sunny February afternoon as Alan Ball's men kicked off a game they were expected to lose on current form. With 14 defeats from 26 league matches to that point, plus failing to score in almost half of those games, it's understandable why few of the 31,115 crowd that day could have envisaged the football feast about to unfurl before their eyes.

The Blues were still struggling to recover from their awful start to the season during which they failed to win any of their first 11 Premier League games. In that same period, Newcastle had won all of their games and opened up a huge lead at the top – talk about contrasting fortunes, not to mention a 33-point gap! Yet this match was to prove that there wasn't a great deal between the two teams when the Blues actually fulfilled the potential that had been bubbling under the surface all season.

City, robbed of several key first-teamers including Garry Flitcroft, Peter Beagrie, Richard Edghill, Terry Phelan and Ian Brightwell through either injury or suspension, had full-back Scott Hiley making his debut and several other players who were on the periphery of the squad.

Yet despite the seemingly weakened XI, it was soon clear from the opening exchanges that City were up for the challenge with Georgi Kinkladze in majestic form.

As the two success-starved giants threw gentle jabs at each other, it was City who deservedly took the lead on 16 minutes.

Hiley made an impressive run down the wing and cut the ball back to Nigel Clough whose vicious low drive clipped Niall Quinn's heel and the ball spun agonisingly over the stranded Pavel Srnicek. There was a moment's silence and then a deafening roar as the ball nestled in the back of the net sending the packed Maine Road wild with delight.

Kinkladze was masterful, displaying the full range of his vast array of skills in midfield. The Magpies could do little to stop the little genius in this mood.

Yet, despite the hosts' dominance, City failed to add to their lead and paid the price on 44 minutes when Belgian centre-half Philippe Albert volleyed home a cracking drive from ten yards.

The second half was 15 minutes old when the battle between the volatile Faustino Asprilla and City skipper Keith Curle finally boiled over.

Asprilla's blatant elbow caught Curle full in the face but the referee either didn't see it or buckled under pressure and ignored it – a straight red should have been brandished but instead tempers were allowed to boil over – to City's cost later in the game. Two minutes later, justice was seen to be done. Kinkladze was at the heart of City's second on 62 minutes as he weaved in, out and mesmerised the visitors' defence before whipping in a low shot that Srnicek did well to keep out.

Kinky gathered the rebound and chipped the ball perfectly to the far post for Quinn to gleefully head home his fifth of the season and second of the game.

City tried to kill the game off with a quick third, but Keegan's irrepressible Magpies were soon back on level terms.

Albert, giving a masterful exhibition of attacking defence, pinged in a low cross-shot that Eike Immel could only parry allowing Asprilla – who should have been having an early bath – to screw the ball home from a tight angle for 2-2. It was a bitter pill for the players and the home fans to swallow.

Back came City again. Steve Lomas crossed from the right wing and Uwe Rosler steered home his sixth of the campaign with only 14 minutes to go and Maine Road once more erupted – surely, that was the end of the goal-feast?

Depressingly, it would be the only time that season that the Blues managed to score more than two goals. The defensive frailties that had haunted Ball's team all season would soon rear their head again and just five minutes later it was 3-3.

Newcastle's man-of-the-match Albert drilled a low drive in which deflected off Quinn and into the net for his second of the game and the sixth of a breathtaking afternoon.

Both teams had chances to win the game, but overall, a draw was a fair result on a day when Kinkladze and Albert lifted those assembled, if only briefly, to a higher plane.

v Wolves 2-1

28 December 1981
First Division
Attendance: 40,298

MANCHESTER CITY:	WOLVERHAMPTON WANDERERS:
Corrigan	Bradshaw
Ranson	Palmer
Wilson	Parkin
Reid	Daniel
Bond	Gallagher
Caton	Berry,
Kinsey	Birch (Matthews)
Reeves	Eves
Francis	Gray
Hartford	Richards
Hutchison	Brazier

THIS MATCH is not an obvious contender for such a grand title as 'greatest game', or even to make the top 60. Yet there was a sprinkling of magical dust that makes it stick in the memory of those who were there on the day.

There are reasons, but flick through the history books and games like this tend to slip between the cracks, all but forgotten in the fullness of time because it had no particular relevance in the grander scheme of things.

In years to come, it will slip further down the pecking order and will eventually be forgotten, but for now, it earns a place in the top 60, and here's why.

Festive programmes have, by and large, been fairly happy times for City over the years. The Blues often play well around the Christmas and New Year period when the league games come fast and furious and John Bond's team approached Christmas 1981 with more than a tinge of optimism with early December victories over Aston Villa at Maine Road and Coventry City at Highfield Road elevating the club to seventh in the First Division table. Dizzy heights for a club that had been rooted to the foot of the table a little more than 12 months earlier.

It was a remarkable turnaround by City who had been marooned at the bottom of the table with only four points from a possible 33. Bond had left the comfortable surrounds of Norwich to test his mettle in the long running soap opera that was Manchester City Football Club.

Bond had performed miracles to take the club up the table and all the way to the Centenary FA Cup Final the previous May while steering the club to a comfortable mid-table finish in the process.

City fans dared to dream the Blues might kick on again for the 1981/82 campaign and if the form of the final five months of the previous campaign could be replicated, there was every chance City would be competing nearer the top of the table rather than the bottom.

A marquee signing was needed to register a statement of intent and for once, chairman Peter Swales delivered. Superstar Trevor Francis was signed in late August from Nottingham Forest and the England striker added a touch of class to an already-decent team that included Kevin Reeves, Tommy Hutchison and Asa Hartford.

As a result, City were a much steadier side during the first half of the campaign, capable of beating anyone on their day.

Pushing for a place in the top four as Christmas approached, the last game before the holiday period augured well for City – a home clash with rock-bottom Sunderland and for most of the match, things seemed to be going to plan.

A brace from Francis had given City a 2-1 lead – an advantage maintained until the dying embers of the game, but the Black Cats, punching well above their weight, somehow clawed their way back from the dead with two goals in the dying seconds to turn the game on its head to win 3-2 and cast doubts among the faithful that Bond's team could seriously challenge for the title. Sunderland had failed to read the script.

A win would have put the Blues in fourth position, just two points shy of leaders Swansea, but the great unpredictables had proved they were capable of pretty much anything on the day depending on their mood. Still, Bond's men remained in the mix and still in seventh in what was proving to be the most open title race for many years.

A daunting Boxing Day trip to Anfield, where City had failed to win in the league since 1953, hardly inspired confidence after such a galling defeat to the Wearsiders and most Blues accepted this would be the usual fruitless trip to the red half of Merseyside, but, as Britain shivered in freezing conditions of snow and ice, the Blues gave their supporters a belated Christmas present in the form of a stunning 3-1 victory over Liverpool.

Admittedly the Reds were some way off their best having won just six of their opening 16 games and Anfield was suddenly pregnable and a long way from being the fortress it had been for a decade or more, but this was a special result for City fans who had become used to the ritual thrashing both home and away to the Reds.

The win pushed City into fourth place, just two points behind Swansea and with most of the holiday programme once again postponed a couple of days later, Maine Road's under-soil heating presented Bond's men with a rare chance to top the table.

A holiday crowd of more than 40,000 packed into the ground for the visit of Wolves who may have been struggling near the foot of the table, but had enjoyed two wins in their previous four visits to Maine Road and were viewed by the home support as very much a bogey side.

Injury to Bobby McDonald presented Clive Wilson with his first-team debut while another youngster, Steve Kinsey, was making his home bow.

Everyone knew a win would take City to the summit and so the tension was almost tangible as the match kicked off. The crowd's anxiety seemed to filter through to the players and mistakes were made, passes over-hit and there was a general disjointedness to the Blues' play.

Wolves began brightly and slowly took command of the match in difficult conditions, holding their own comfortably and occasionally threatening to break the deadlock.

The scrappy first period ended 0-0 and Bond led his troops into the dressing room for a dressing down and as a result, City re-emerged looking more focused and determined not to the lose the opportunity of leading the tightly-packed First Division into the New Year.

With only eight minutes of the second half gone, the breakthrough finally came. Hartford drilled his second goal in three days to put the Blues 1-0 up and the relief was palpable – at least while it lasted.

Wolves were in no mood to ease City's path to the top and thanks to an eagle-eyed linesman, they were presented with a chance of staging a late recovery when Joe Corrigan was adjudged to have stepped outside his area while making a clearance upfield.

The Wolverhampton players, once again tapping in to the Blues' anxiety and feeling of injustice, made the most of the incident as the home side appeared to momentarily switch off. Ray Daniel drove the free kick low and hard and Corrigan watched in horror as the ball skidded off his hands and into the net for a deserved equaliser.

Wolves then lived up to their name and moved in for the kill. City were hanging on with defenders Tommy Caton and Kevin Bond particularly outstanding, but when striker Mel Eaves claimed his angled shot had crossed the line a few minutes later, Maine Road held its collective breath and expected the worst.

Clive Wilson, hugely impressive on his debut, had seemingly managed to scramble the ball to safety and the referee agreed with the linesman that the whole of the ball had not crossed the line, much to the chagrin of the visitors who protested vehemently against the decision. Well, given their plight, they would!

Surely even City wouldn't suffer back-to-back defeats to teams at the bottom of the league?

Though out of sorts, the Blues were still in the game and with five minutes to go, Francis, largely anonymous throughout the match, showed why City had splashed out more than a million pounds on his undoubted match-winning qualities. Corrigan launched a mighty clearance into the Wolves half and defender George Berry could only direct his header into Francis's path.

Francis took half-a-dozen steps forward and lashed a thunderous drive into the back of the net from the edge of the box. Maine Road erupted and this time the Blues held out in the final nervous moments to win 2-1.

The celebrations at the final whistle were testament enough to how the City fans felt about topping the table for the first time in four years. There was still a long way to go but just 14 months earlier the Blues had been rooted to the foot of the table and looked like relegation certainties so there was some justification in the post-match hyperbole.

Bond said later, 'I must have aged four years, although I'd feel worse if I were the Wolves manager and had lost after playing so well. Trevor Francis will never score another goal like that even if he lives to be 150, but then, that's why he's a million pound player.'

Years later Francis revealed that whenever he returned to face the Blues as a player or a manager, everyone recalled the winning goal he scored for them and the impact he had on the team.

'I've scored better goals and certainly more important ones,' he said, 'but the City fans have never forgotten it and always remind me of it whenever I'm back in Manchester. For that reason alone, it is a special goal.'

City enjoyed life at the top and maintained their challenge at the top for a month, but then faded away badly as Bond's magic began to wear off.

Injuries to Francis didn't help and perhaps the team began to believe it couldn't win without his influence. Just three wins in the final 17 games meant the side that had topped the table going into 1982 had finished a disappointing tenth by the end of the season with the form of a relegation side – an almost complete reversal of the previous campaign.

The dip in form had been a precursor for the following season where City continued to deteriorate, particularly with Francis sold on barely 12 months after signing and when Bond quit after a 4-0 FA Cup thrashing away to Brighton, the writing was on the wall.

Despite there being more than three months of the season to go, a doomed City slipped closer and closer to the trap door only to be relegated on the final day of the season in the most dramatic circumstances imaginable.

A 1-0 home defeat to Luton meant City dropped into the bottom three for the first time just four minutes from the end of the campaign.

Still, the goal from Francis against Wolves and the league table the following day had, at least, given the City fans a warm glow for a few days.

4 v Leicester City 1-0

26 April 1969
FA Cup Final, Wembley Stadium
Attendance: 100,000

MANCHESTER CITY:	LEICESTER CITY:
Dowd	Shilton
Book	Rodrigues
Pardoe	Nish
Doyle	Roberts
Booth	Woollett
Oakes	Cross
Summerbee	Fern
Bell	Gibson
Lee	Lochhead
Coleman	Clarke
Young	Glover (Manley 70)

LONG BEFORE the days of the Premier League and Champions League, there were only two prizes most English footballers wanted to win – the First Division title and the FA Cup.

If the former was the equivalent to a marathon, the latter was most certainly the blue ribbon sprint and the prestige of lifting world football's oldest domestic trophy was second to none and the stuff of a million boyhood dreams.

For City, it had been too long since the last FA Cup Final when Bert Trautmann won the hearts of a nation as well as the cup for the Blues as he played the last 20 minutes of the 1956 occasion with a broken neck.

Since then, there had been nothing and apart from the league title won the year before, there had been precious little else for City fans to cheer. Yet there was a feeling during the 1968/69 season that the Blues' name could be on the cup.

So abject had City's title defence been, it seemed the players – virtually the same XI that had won the league with such a swagger – decided the FA Cup represented a very acceptable consolation prize.

The cup run had brought the very best out of Joe Mercer's men and was a shot at redemption – proof that the best team in the land had actually just lost their way somewhere in the bread and butter of league football.

Leicester City were the opposition in the final and the teams had already met twice in the league that season, with the Foxes beating the defending champions 3-0 at Filbert Street and City winning the return game 2-0 courtesy of a Mike Summerbee brace.

The Blues had been struggling in mid-table for most of the campaign and had suffered an embarrassing first round exit in the European Cup to Turkish side Fenerbahce – this after coach Malcolm Allison had promised his team would 'terrify Europe'.

Still, there had been the odd flashes of genius along the way and Mercer's men still had the capacity to enchant the nation by turning on the style occasionally. As Christmas approached, City beat West Brom 5-1, Burnley 7-0 and Coventry City 4-2.

As far as the title was concerned, it was too little, too late, with the damage done in the early months of the season when the Blues clearly had trouble shaking their title hangover. The team accepted their fate and instead turned their attention to the last piece of silverware they could still win.

There was little to suggest there would be anything special about this cup run as the Blues began their quest with an unconvincing 1-0 win over Luton Town at Maine Road courtesy of a Francis Lee goal in front of 37,120 fans.

Playing well within themselves and against opposition who were worthy of the somewhat patronising tag of 'plucky', City went into the hat at the expense of the Hatters.

The draw for the next round, however, was not so kind with a difficult-looking trip to St James' Park to face Newcastle United where just eight months earlier City had dramatically clinched the championship with an exhilarating 4-3 win the previous May – but a venue where they had already lost 1-0 in the league fixture a couple of months earlier.

With more than 55,000 packed in and the Gallowgate End in full voice, Mercer and Allison knew that this was a game in which a similar gung-ho attitude would likely end in defeat and effectively end the season.

The return of skipper Tony Book, who had missed the first half of the campaign with an Achilles injury, could not have been timed any better and City proved resilient and difficult to break down.

They left the north-east with a deserved, hard-fought 0-0 draw and finished the job off four days later with a 2-0 win in front of a massive Maine Road crowd of 60,844 – this despite playing most of the game with only ten men following Summerbee's early red card.

One step closer to the twin towers and into the last 16, the fifth round saw City paired with Second Division Blackburn Rovers at Ewood Park and given an excellent chance of progressing to the quarter-finals.

The freezing February weather put paid to several league fixtures and this was City's first game for a month, but there were no signs of rust as two goals each from Tony Coleman and Lee put the Blues within sight of Wembley following a resounding 4-1 win. The momentum, it appeared, was peaking at exactly the right time.

Now only Tottenham Hotspur stood between the Blues and a place in the semi-finals with the famous ballet on ice from the previous season now a distant memory.

In front of nearly 50,000 Maine Road fans it was again Lee who grabbed the only goal of a tightly-contested match.

March was proving an enjoyable month for the Blue half of Manchester with Summerbee securing a 1-0 win over United at Old Trafford in the derby to at least secure the bragging rights at league level, while the draw for the semis pitted the Blues with cup favourites Everton.

The Manchester and Merseyside Blues had already met twice in the league and the Toffees had won them both. For many, it was the final itself, with the two best teams remaining knowing that the winners would be in with a terrific chance of going on and winning the competition.

The tie was played at Villa Park in front of 63,025 and proved a tactical battle with both teams cancelling each other out for long periods. City defended stoutly and though forced to weather long periods of Everton pressure, stood firm as the game appeared to be heading for a replay.

Then, with seconds remaining, Tommy Booth popped up to score his second goal of the season – a dramatic winner to send the Blues to Wembley and around 30,000 City fans into raptures. There was no way back for the Toffees and the final whistle blew moments later.

A backlog of fixtures meant five league games in 15 days and hardly surprisingly, a tired City team lost three of the matches, including a clash with leaders Leeds United a day after a 2-0 home win over cup final opponents Leicester City.

Cup fever had gripped Manchester and all the tickets were sold soon after going on sale but the Blues' form going into the final was an ongoing concern with successive defeats at West Brom and Southampton hardly inspiring confidence.

City needed a touch of arrogance – anything – to put the spark back into the game and a typical yet subtle piece of Allison psychology seemed to do the trick as time came to head out of the dressing rooms and prepare for the game.

Allison told his players to hang back for a minute or two to deliberately keep the Leicester players waiting in the tunnel. Finally, the City players emerged and lined up alongside their opponents before walking out to the deafening roar of 100,000 fans.

It was a proud moment for both Joe Mercer and Leicester boss Frank O'Farrell as they led their teams out for the jewel in the crown of English football's domestic season.

For Leicester in particular, reaching the final had been a triumph over adversity after having the shock result of the competition by beating Liverpool 1-0 at Anfield earlier in the competition. That was even more impressive considering they had lost 16 games away from home in the league and would be relegated just two weeks after the final.

The Blues quickly turned on the style, attacking from the start but Leicester, revelling in their role as underdogs, grew in confidence and created chances of their own as the match ebbed and flowed.

The Foxes were playing their third Wembley final of the decade and were determined not to make it an unwanted hat-trick with a third defeat in succession and both Clarke and Rodrigues had opportunities to give the East Midlands outfit the lead – Clarke seeing his shot brilliantly saved by Harry Dowd and Rodrigues somehow missing a chance from a couple of yards out as he sliced the ball wide from close range.

Just three minutes after that miss, they were made to pay a heavy price as City finally broke the deadlock.

Summerbee wriggled past lunging challenges from Nish and Woollett down the right before pulling the ball back from the byline where it rolled perfectly into the path of the on-rushing Neil Young to fire an unstoppable shot past Peter Shilton and into the roof of the net and give his team a 1-0 lead.

Dowd preserved City's slender advantage with several fine saves after the break and was the Blues' outstanding performer on the day – the fact that he was the man of the match proves Leicester were more than a tad unfortunate on the day, but despite their best efforts, City hung on to claim a memorable win – Mercer's men had their names on the cup all along.

Years later, Mike Doyle recalled the feeling among the team that had driven the Blues to glory.

He said, 'I could tell by the attitude of the lads we were going to win the FA Cup. After we beat Everton in the semi-final, nobody could have stopped us. We didn't consider Leicester, our opponents in the final, as any great shakes, either.

'No one talked about the possibility of beating Leicester – it was a case of "when", not "if". I didn't get any butterflies until we were driving down Wembley Way.

'When I saw all the fans milling around the Twin Towers, it hit me like a sledgehammer and that in 90 minutes, all those people would be inside and waiting for the game to kick off.

'Everything changed when we walked down the tunnel with only one thought – to win another trophy for our fans.'

Doyle also has one painful recollection from that momentous day. He says, 'During the game, Leicester took a free kick and it hit me in a rather sensitive place!

'The camera must have zoomed in on my face because I remember swearing in exasperation. The next day my mum said, "Michael, we never brought you up to use language like that"!

'She was obviously better at lip-reading than I'd given her credit for!'

As HRH Princess Anne handed the FA Cup over to skipper Tony Book, the former Bath City full-back must have been pinching himself.

'Skip' had been playing Southern League football for Bath just five years earlier and now he was holding aloft the most famous cup in the world as captain of the Blues – could life get any better?

5 v AC Milan 2-2

23 November 1978
UEFA Cup third round first leg

MANCHESTER CITY:	AC MILAN:
Corrigan	Albertosi
Clements	Collovati
Donachie	Maidera
Booth	Bet
Watson	Baresi
Power	Di Vacchi
Viljoen (Keegan)	Buriani
Bell	Bigon
Kidd	Novellino
Hartford	Rivera
Channon	Chiodi

ON A surreal Thursday afternoon in Italy, City played AC Milan and came within a whisker of creating history in the San Siro – but first the explanation behind the early kick-off and unusual Thursday fixture. City had flown to Italy to face one of European football's traditional powerhouses and a team already leading a very competitive domestic league.

The Blues were out of sorts in their own competition and a long way from the side that had challenged for the title in recent campaigns. Five league games without a win going into this match would become 13 without maximum points stretching almost four months.

In fact, City had become one of the teams of the 1970s after finishing runners-up to Liverpool at the end of the 1976/77 campaign – by a single point – and fourth in 1977/78. It was the latter finish that guaranteed a UEFA Cup berth as City sought to improve their recent mixed fortunes in Europe that had seen a first-round exit in the European Cup followed by a European Cup Winners' Cup success.

After reaching the semi-final of the same competition a year later and then failing in the early rounds of European competitions twice more in the mid-1970s, the Blues had been fairly regular competitors in Europe but had a very much hit-and-miss success rate.

After narrowly seeing off Dutch side FC Twente in the first round and then comfortably eliminating Belgian outfit Standard Liege, hopes were high that this season progression to the latter stages might be a possibility – with a bit of luck along the way.

The draw was one of the toughest the Blues could have possibly had – save for favourites Borussia Monchengladbach – and on paper it looked like it would go to form and yet another European adventure would end prematurely.

Milan were flying, conceded few goals and had a great record against English opposition. There was hope, though, as the Italians hadn't won Serie A for 11 years and had gone through nine managers in seven years as they sought a return to the glory years of the late 1960s that had seen them crowned European champions in 1969.

But a glance at the team sheet is evidence enough that Tony Book's side was packed with internationals and quality and if the stars aligned, anything was possible.

The match had originally been due to start the evening before on Wednesday, but despite everyone being good to go, the Milanese weather had other ideas and when thick fog descended on the magnificent San Siro just a few hours before kick-off, the officials had no choice but to call the match off.

Images of Book and chairman Peter Swales walking off the pitch surrounded by an ethereal mist is testament to what a classic 'pea-souper' it was!

Desperate measures were needed when no obvious date jumped out for the match to be rescheduled and, considering everyone was in the right place so to speak, all parties agreed that the following afternoon was ideal – something that today's television moguls would surely never sanction.

The viewing figures for a Thursday afternoon match would be right down there alongside the re-runs of *Heartbeat* and *Cash In the Attic*, but in a rare act of common sense, on 23 November 1978 Manchester City ran out to the glorious sight of one of the world's best venues, bathed in warm, early afternoon autumn sunshine.

Just a handful of the 1,000 or so Blues that had made the journey to Italy stayed on for the game which still managed to attract a huge gate of 60,000, but the atmosphere was less hostile – the crowd was more muted and there were no firecrackers to be heard or flares to be seen. The uniqueness of the European midweek atmosphere was absent and City used it to their advantage.

Milan were imperious inside the San Siro and had never lost to a British side on their own turf. They had won six and drawn two of the games against English opposition and were strong favourites to continue that record.

Despite City's decidedly average season, victories in the previous rounds against FC Twente and Standard Liege proved the team were capable of adapting to a more European style, but Milan were a couple of notches up on the teams met so far.

Predictably, Milan started by putting City immediately under pressure, and while the Italians never missed an opportunity to ruffle City's feathers, either verbally, physically or by trying to convince the referee the challenge they had just been on the end of had resulted in a near death experience, they found the towering central defensive partnership of Tommy Booth and Dave Watson in superb form.

The hosts' frustration steadily grew after failing to find an early breakthrough. Asa Hartford was starting to boss things in the middle and when the industrious Scot picked up the ball on the left-hand side of the Milan box, he floated a perfect cross to the far post and Brian Kidd powerfully headed into the opposite corner to leave the keeper flat-footed and give the Blues an unlikely lead.

With virtually no City vocal support left inside the San Siro, Milan came back strongly and had the ball in the net almost straight from the re-start, but it was ruled out for offside.

Unbelievably, the lunchtime kick-off meant that as the half-time whistle blew, the majority of City fans had to leave the stadium to catch their plane home! It was cruel to say the least, but at least they had seen Kidd's goal before setting off for the airport. Had they known what was to come next, chances are they would have paid for a later flight home.

City weathered frantic pressure as the Italians fought to stay in the tie, but in the 57th minute, the Blues again silenced the home crowd by doubling the lead.

Paul Power picked the ball up just outside his own area and then carried the ball forward and down the right flank. Pretty much unchallenged, he continued to the edge of the Milan box before feigning to shoot and cutting inside before firing a fairly weak shot on goal that bobbled before deceiving Albertosi and nestling in the net to make it 2-0 – it was incredible stuff and typical that there were no City fans to see it either in the flesh or live on TV!

The Blues needed to get the ball and kill the game for the next 15 minutes if they were to pull off a famous win but instead, perhaps giddy at the scoreline, they let Milan pull one back almost straight from the kick-off through Bigon – the worst possible scenario.

Bigon had the ball in the net again four minutes later as Book's side suddenly looked very vulnerable and decidedly edgy, but the linesman's flag came to the rescue once again and it was ruled offside.

That should have served as the wake-up call the Blues needed, but the Italians were building up an impressive head of steam and their volatile fans, stirred by the comeback, began throwing missiles at Joe Corrigan in the City goal as the atmosphere finally cranked into life.

It seemed inevitable that Milan would draw level at some point and on 83 minutes, they finally did thanks again to Bigon. A hopeful pass to the edge of the box should have been cleared but it instead somehow found its way through to the Milan striker and he made no mistake from close range.

Thoughts of victory banished, the Blues were forced to hang on for a still impressive draw as Milan pressed for a winner, but there were no more goals and the game ended 2-2.

It was still a fantastic result and one of the Blues' best in European football – but a chance had been missed, all the same. There was, however, even better to come.

City went for broke in the return leg at Maine Road and systematically took the Serie A giants apart on an occasion that would prove to be one of the greatest European nights the City fans would ever witness.

In 45 breathtaking minutes, City scored three times without reply and this time there was to be no Milan comeback. There was no further scoring after the break as the Blues sent out a powerful message, winning the tie 5-2 on aggregate to move into the UEFA Cup quarter-finals.

As a measure of the achievement against Milan, the Italians went on to win the Serie A title, losing just three league games all season and never conceding more than two goals in any of their fixtures.

The Milan win should have given the team the confidence to go on and perhaps even win the cup, but another unfortunate draw saw City paired with favourites Borussia Monchengladbach and the tie was as good as over after a 1-1 draw at Maine Road and a 3-1 loss in Germany meant a 4-2 aggregate defeat.

It was to be Tony Book's last season in charge and City finished in 15th position, crashing out of the FA Cup to Third Division minnows Shrewsbury Town along the way to complete a fairly miserable campaign.

Nobody, however, would forget the memory of Milan, though many would question how such a high could be achieved over two matches against the Rossoneri when there had been so many abject performances elsewhere.

6 v West Bromwich A 2-1

7 March 1970
League Cup Final, Wembley Stadium
Attendance: 97,963

MANCHESTER CITY:	WEST BROMWICH ALBION:
Corrigan	Osborne
Book	Fraser
Mann	Wilson
Doyle	Brown
Booth	Talbut
Oakes	Kaye
Heslop	Cantello
Bell	Suggett
Summerbee (Bowyer)	Astle
Lee	Hartford (Krzywicki)
Pardoe	Hope

WITH A league title in 1968 and the FA Cup in 1969, City were desperate to keep their run of at least one trophy per season and making it to the 1970 League Cup Final offered the perfect opportunity to do exactly that.

It was City's first final in the competition which had begun just a decade earlier and it was easily the highest profile game against West Bromwich Albion.

It was also, memorably, played on a muddy, initially snow-covered Wembley pitch famously described by Blues' manager Joe Mercer as 'a pig of a pitch' – the surface resembling that of a potato patch, grassless, bumpy and sticky underfoot.

It was a long way short of the bowling-green surface everybody had come to expect of England's home stadium but it was hardly surprising given that the Horse of the Year Show had been held at Wembley just days earlier – an unthinkable scenario in today's world where perfection is demanded from players, sponsors and a global audience of millions. The horses had cut the pitch up and the wintry weather had done the rest.

However, the fact that so many volunteers had cleared the snow that had fallen overnight, plus the slight rise in temperature, meant referee James passed the game fit to play.

This was to be a gruelling game for City, backed by 34,000 fans and playing in their famous red and black striped kit, not only because West Brom were obviously a good side having recorded a 3-0 win at The Hawthorns over the Blues just five weeks before, but because of the circumstances surrounding the run-up to the final.

Three days earlier, City had ground out a 0-0 draw in the European Cup Winners' Cup quarter-final away to Portuguese outfit Academica Coimbra. It had been a draining 90 minutes against a hard-working, young team and the journey home had been long and tiring with thick fog meaning the team's flight had to divert from London to the Midlands and make the rest of the journey by coach.

For the players, it seemed events were conspiring against them as they started their bid for a third major trophy in three years.

Albion were safe from relegation in the lower half of the table and had seen off Carlisle United in the semi-final while City had beaten Manchester United over two epic legs, 2-1 at Maine Road and 2-2 at Old Trafford.

Neil Young was a notable absentee from the team that ran out to face the Baggies and Arthur Mann was handed a rare start as a result with Glyn Pardoe pushing into midfield.

City were soon on the rack and fell behind to a Jeff Astle header on six minutes after Joe Corrigan and George Heslop got in each other's way – Heslop stepping on Corrigan's foot as it happened – but it only served to be the wake-up call the Blues needed.

Slowly, City began to stifle Albion with Heslop and Booth giving little away at the back and the inspirational Alan Oakes and Mike Doyle surging forward at every opportunity from midfield. Try as they might, however, there would be no further scoring in the first half as West Brom went in for their half-time cuppa with their precious lead intact.

The Black Country outfit should have all-but sealed victory shortly after the re-start when Colin Suggett broke free of the City back four but he made a hash of the chance and was left to rue what might have been.

Soon after, City punished that miss after winning a corner on the hour-mark. Mike Summerbee flicked on the corner to Colin Bell who cushioned a header into Mike Doyle's path and the Blues' half-back sent in a first-time shot that beat Osborne and City, at last, were level.

The question was, with the pitch sapping energy from the players as the game wore on, did the Blues have enough gas in the tank to see the task through?

It was now anybody's game and City's quest was about to get even harder as Summerbee had to be substituted after sustaining a hairline fracture of his leg. No Young and no Summerbee – the balance on the flanks was gone and the momentum seemed to be tipping back towards West Brom.

Future City favourite Asa Hartford, who was then playing for West Brom, was substituted late in normal time and his replacement Krzywicki used his pace to almost grab a dramatic winner for the Midlands outfit then Franny Lee went close for City shortly after, but a result in normal time just wasn't to be and the game went into extra time – the last thing Mercer's men needed.

With the watching nation now expecting the marginally fresher West Brom to finish the job off, the exhausted Blues somehow dug deep into their reserves and showed the spirit that had made them champions just a couple of years earlier as they conjured up what proved to be a 102nd-minute winner.

Lee chipped a ball to Bell in the box and his back-heel fell perfectly for Pardoe. He looked up, shot and squeezed a drive past the Baggies keeper from the corner of the box to send the travelling Mancunians wild. There were no further goals and Tony Book lifted the trophy for the first time in City's history.

It was the first time the League Cup had come to the north-west and – more significantly – it was the very first time that all 92 clubs of the Football League had taken part, making the triumph all the more sweet.

Less than two months later, City added the European Cup Winners' Cup to the Maine Road trophy cabinet to complete a memorable period of success for the club.

v Tottenham Hotspur 4-3

4 February 2004
FA Cup fourth round replay
Attendance: 30,400

MANCHESTER CITY:	TOTTENHAM HOTSPUR:
Arason	Keller
Sun	Carr
Tarnat	Richards
Distin	Gardner
Dunne	Ziege (Jackson 60)
Bosvelt	Dalmat
Wright-Phillips	King
Barton	Brown
Sinclair (McManaman 80)	Davies
Anelka (Macken 27)	Postiga (Poyet 9)
Fowler (Sibierski 80)	Keane

I
T WAS a match that was, quite simply, unforgettable, breathtaking and in terms of sheer theatre, incredible. For many, it was quintessential Kevin Keegan, with goals, drama, excitement and controversy in almost equal measure and a night that seemed to have sunk City fans' hearts to the deepest pits of despair ended with scenes of disbelief, elation and ecstasy.

For the Blues' beleaguered manager, this game was manna from heaven. The odds were stacked against the Blues following a disastrous run of just one win in 18 matches and in any language that amounted to one thing – relegation form. The Keegan magic had faded to a dull lustre and he seemed no longer capable of rallying his badly mis-firing team.

They needed a boost from somewhere – anywhere – before the damage became irreversible, though after the first 45 minutes of this match at White Hart Lane, it looked like the former England manager might be on the verge of holding his hands up and passing the reins on to somebody else.

For many, the first clash between these two sides at the City of Manchester Stadium had offered the Blues the best chance of progressing into the fifth round. A 1-1 draw suggested that chance had passed and within only two minutes of the replay in North London, City faced a monumental challenge as Ledley King showed a sleight of foot not usually associated with central defenders as he cut inside Jihai Sun and fired a spectacular shot past Arnie Arason into the roof of the net.

There was worse to come for City, too. Robbie Keane latched on to a superb through ball on 19 minutes, controlling the pass and then lifting the ball over Arason to make it 2-0 and then Nicholas Anelka limped off with just 27 minutes played – surely the Blues' night couldn't get any worse?

Joey Barton's over-the-top challenge on Michael Brown a couple of minutes before the break earned him a yellow card and from the resulting free kick Christian Ziege curled a beautiful shot into the top corner to put the hosts – it appeared – into the next round.

The whistle blew for half-time but Rob Styles's work wasn't over as Barton continued to argue about his booking. Despite warnings from the referee, he persisted and was shown the red card as the rest of the team made its way down the tunnel.

Down to ten men, trailing 3-0 and playing terribly – no wonder Keegan's hair had gone grey.

Damage limitation seemed the order of the day. Spurs looked set for a cricket score and a five- or six-goal thrashing could have spelled the end for the Blues' enigmatic manager.

But something strange happened. City came out and began to play football and it seemed to take Spurs back a little. If fortune really did favour the brave, the Blues were going to have to dig deep within their reserves of courage and derring-do if they were to salvage a little pride and when a free kick was awarded 40 yards out just three minutes after the break, a chance to repair some of the damage presented itself.

The excellent Michael Tarnat floated the ball towards the six-yard box where Spurs, perhaps too cocksure, allowed a galloping Sylvain Distin enough space to fashion a header – of sorts – past Kasey Keller to make it 3-1.

Not long after Spurs came within a whisker of making it 4-1 as Ziege fired in another superb free kick, only to see it strike the bar and Keane miss the chance to head home the rebound as Arason scrambled back to stop the ball on the line. Arason, making his debut for City, was immense and would make another two incredible saves to keep the hosts at bay.

With almost 70 minutes gone, City were still clinging on at 3-1 down. As the ball was cleared by the Spurs defence, Paul Bosvelt hit a low drive that span wickedly off Anthony Gardner and past Keller to make it 3-2. Suddenly the White Hart Lane crowd sounded anxious and the players responded accordingly, mis-placing passes and looking increasingly nervous.

The 1,500 or so City fans who had made the journey south roared on their ten men and, with ten minutes to go, Shaun Wright-Phillips was put clean through and as Keller raced off his line, he lifted the ball gently past him to make it 3-3. It was a fantastic comeback and even if Spurs had grabbed a winner, proved the team were capable of much better things, but there was still one more twist to come.

With the clock ticking past 90 minutes, City pressed for an unlikely winner. Extra time beckoned and for the home team, a chance to regroup and restore sanity.

The ball was deep in the Spurs half when it found its way to Tarnat. The cultured German lifted a cross towards the back post where Jon Macken had an awful lot to do, but the former Preston man leapt up, made a terrific connection and then watched as his header sailed past Keller and into the net – cue pandemonium.

The City fans, players and management went wild and the Tottenham players looked at each other in total disbelief. How could they have thrown it away? Three goals up, 45 minutes to play and the opposition down to ten men.

The whistle went moments later, completing one of the greatest comebacks of all time and one of the most exciting FA Cup matches ever.

As Keegan succinctly pointed out afterwards, 'They'll be talking about this match long after we've all gone.'

Fortunately, most of us are still here, Kev, but we are, indeed, still talking about it.

v Newcastle United 5-1

18 January 1975
First Division
Attendance: 32,021

MANCHESTER CITY:	NEWCASTLE UNITED:
Corrigan	McFaul
Hammond	Nattrass
Donachie	Kennedy
Doyle	Smith
Booth	Keeley
Oakes	Howard
Bell	Howard
Summerbee	Nulty
Marsh	Macdonald
Tueart	Tudor (Barrowclough)
Royle	Craig

AS A seven-year-old Noel Gallagher trundled into Maine Road for the first time with his dad, the Blues were preparing for a home league game with Newcastle United who had won an FA Cup tie 2-0 on the same ground just a fortnight earlier.

City had actually drawn the Magpies away in the third round but due to an FA ruling following a breach of the rules by the north-east giants, the game was played at Maine Road.

Advantage City? Of course not – the Blues, mentally at least, still played as though they were at St James' Park as they meekly went out of the competition at the first hurdle.

Add the cup exit to a 2-1 defeat at St James' Park just six weeks before in the league and Tony Book's side had all the motivation they needed to put the Magpies to the sword – or did the black and whites have the Indian Sign over City?

It was an intriguing match, if for no other reason than the spectacular inconsistency – even by City's standards – shown in the previous months.

When Book's side had clicked during the 1974/75 campaign, they did so with conviction and style, often blowing teams out of the water with consummate ease. In fact, the Blues had begun the season with a 4-0 win over West Ham and were the early pace-setters in the First Division before enduring a few hiccups on the road and a miserable festive period that included losses to Liverpool and Derby County.

The Blues were very much a team in transition with Franny Lee sold to Derby County (and scoring a scorcher at Maine Road in the aforementioned festive flop – Barry Davies crowed on *Match of the Day*, 'Look at his face, just look at his face!') and Mike Summerbee was also now on the transfer list as his time in sky blue neared an end.

Book was carefully assembling his own team from the ashes of the Joe Mercer and Malcolm Allison era and with so many ageing crowd favourites to move on, it was never going to be easy.

There were good days and bad along the way but overall, the green shoots of recovery were sprouting after a topsy-turvy 1973/74 season when the Blues had employed three different managers.

Out of both cup competitions but despite being in eighth position in the First Division, City were not necessarily out of the title race, trailing leaders Ipswich Town by just three points.

It was the Blues' away form that was pegging them back in the league with just one win on the road in 13 games more like relegation form than a club challenging at the top.

At Maine Road, however, City were practically invincible and had won ten, drawn two and lost just one of their 13 matches. Very much a season of contrasts thus far.

As Book recalled years later, 'We just couldn't buy a win away from home. We weren't doing anything differently but we were like two different teams when we played at home and away.'

A disappointing crowd of 32,021 were, nonetheless, hopeful of another home triumph and Book knew if he could crack the puzzle of his team's away day blues, City could still put in a late challenge for the title.

Asa Hartford and Keith MacRae were both missing through injury meaning recalls for the transfer-listed Summerbee and deposed former number one Joe Corrigan.

The game began at a lively pace with both teams eager to get back to winning ways after recent setbacks. Newcastle had conceded five goals in their last game while City had played out a drab 1-1 draw away to Sheffield United, so the first goal was always going to be vital and thankfully, it was

Geoff Hammond who stabbed the ball home to give City the lead with just seven minutes played.

The Magpies roared back with a Malcolm Macdonald thunderbolt levelling the scores on 14 minutes. The match continued to ebb and flow with chances at both ends, but it was a boyhood Newcastle United fan, Dennis Tueart, who restored City's lead on 37 minutes, tucking home a penalty kick for his seventh league goal of the season.

The Blues just about deserved to go in at the break 2-1 up and the second half soon deteriorated into a feisty affair, particularly after Tueart made it 3-1 six minutes after the re-start.

Summerbee clashed with Pat Howard and Rodney Marsh aimed a punch at Mickey Burns that referee Ron Challis decided to ignore as tempers boiled over but as this was a third meeting between the clubs in six weeks, it was understandable that petty feuds would develop.

Nonetheless, City managed to keep their focus and the hapless Geordies were finally put to bed when the brilliant Tueart completed his hat-trick on 84 minutes – his first for the club, though several more would follow.

Colin Bell rubbed salt in the visitors' wounds when he added a fifth two minutes from time to complete an emphatic victory for Book's men and leave future Oasis founder Noel Gallagher smitten for life and probably thinking it was as entertaining as that every week!

With the top eight clubs now separated by just two points, City were very much in the thick of the race for the title, but the rotten away form which had blighted the campaign continued in the next game when City went down 4-0 to Stoke.

So while the home form went from strength to strength – 16 wins from 21, no less – just 11 points from a possible 42 on the road resulted in an eighth place finish, just seven points behind champions Derby County, managed by Dave Mackay.

Had just four away defeats been victories instead, Book might have been celebrating instead of the man he jointly claimed the Footballer of the Year title with in 1969.

v Birmingham City 3-1

5 May 1956
FA Cup Final, Wembley Stadium
Attendance: 100,000

MANCHESTER CITY:	BIRMINGHAM CITY:
Trautmann	Merrick
Leivers	Hall
Little	Green
Barnes	Newman
Ewing	Smith
Paul	Boyd
Johnstone	Astall
Hayes	Kinsey
Revie	Brown
Dyson	Murphy
Clarke	Govan

A TALENTED CITY side returned to Wembley after losing in the final to Newcastle United just 12 months earlier. After defeat to the Magpies, inspirational captain Roy Paul vowed to return the next year and lift the trophy for the Blues.

Remarkably this wasn't the first time a City captain had vowed to lead his men back to the Twin Towers – Sam Cowan had made the same promise after City lost to Everton in the 1933 FA Cup Final – and then returned to Wembley to beat Portsmouth in 1934. Could Paul really re-create history?

City manager Les McDowall had assembled a fantastic team with the likes of Bert Trautmann, Roy Little, Ken Barnes, Dave Ewing and Roy Paul – possibly one of the Blues' greatest-ever defences – among its number.

With the inventive, intelligent and diminutive Bobby Johnstone, Joe Hayes, Don Revie and Roy Clarke in attack, it was surprising that City finished only in fourth place in the First Division that season – no doubt the FA Cup exploits diluted the championship challenge with McDowall's men never able to simply 'concentrate on the league'.

Despite Paul's claim, if the Blues were to repeat the feats of 1934, they were going to have to do it the hard way.

The route to Wembley had been a perilous one beginning in front of 42,517 at Maine Road with a narrow 2-1 victory over Blackpool with goals from Johnstone and Jack Dyson edging out the Seasiders.

The Tangerines had led the division for much of the season but found City to be a thorn in their side having lost at Maine Road in the league already and later in the campaign, City would beat them again at Bloomfield Road to complete a notable hat-trick.

Then, a trip to Roots Hall proved equally tough in the fourth round with Joe Hayes scoring the only goal in front of a capacity 29,500 crowd.

The bumper crowds continued when an amazing 70,640 crammed into Maine Road to see the Blues and Liverpool battle out a 0-0 draw in the fifth round. But though the Second Division Reds had perhaps swung the tie in their favour, order was restored as City won the replay 2-1 at Anfield in front of nearly 58,000 with Hayes and Dyson grabbing the goals.

City then made it a Merseyside double by seeing off Everton in the quarter-finals as goals from Hayes and Johnstone gave the Blues a 2-1 win in front of another packed Maine Road with 76,129 in attendance as cup fever gripped the blue half of Manchester. The soothsayer Paul seemed to be on to something!

By now seemingly unstoppable, City powered past Spurs at Villa Park in the semi-final with Johnstone scoring the only goal on the day in front of just under 70,000, meaning that skipper Paul's promise had been kept. City were once again at the Twin Towers and were in no mood to play the role of bridesmaid.

Only Billy Spurdle was missing from the side that had beaten Spurs as City walked on to the Wembley turf with Birmingham City – a side the Blues had lost 4-3 to at St Andrew's and drawn 1-1 with in the league already that season.

In fact, the Midlands side had been drawn away in all four rounds and had more than earned their place in the final having seen off Torquay, West Brom, Leyton Orient, Arsenal and Sunderland in the semis.

Don Revie replaced the unfortunate Spurdle and would prove to be far more than just an adequate replacement. City had adopted what would later be known as the 'Revie plan' whereby the traditional centre-forward played in a deep role behind two other strikers, making it difficult for centre-halves to pick him up – a plan based on the successful Hungarian national side and also much-criticised the previous year in defeat to Newcastle.

This time, however, it would work a treat and the innovative Blues reaped their reward.

Revie played an integral part in what was to be the perfect start for McDowall's team. His 40-yard pass found Roy Clarke who returned the ball to Revie who then skilfully flicked it into the path of Joe Hayes who slotted home the ball with only three minutes on the clock.

Stunned, Birmingham composed themselves and equalised on 15 minutes through Noel Kinsey and that was the end of the scoring for the first half.

The key to City's triumph came midway through the second half when Dyson was put clear after tremendous work by Revie, Johnstone and Barnes and he made no mistake to restore City's lead.

Two minutes later and the famous old trophy was on its way to Maine Road as Johnstone scored his fourth of the competition to make it 3-1 and send the travelling Mancunians into raptures.

The match, however, will always be best remembered for one man's incredible bravery. Bert Trautmann, City's legendary German goalkeeper, fearlessly saved at Birmingham striker Murphy's feet 15 minutes from time and took a blow to the neck from his knee.

Trautmann, clearly in a great deal of pain, continued to play, despite appearing to have sustained a serious injury. The courage he showed in those final minutes took on the stuff of legend when it was later discovered that the big keeper had broken two bones in his neck and a further knock could have left him in a wheelchair – or worse – for the rest of his days.

It was an incredible act of heroism as there were no substitute goalkeepers on the bench in those days and the reason the 1956 final will always be remembered as Trautmann's final.

v Huddersfield Town 10-1

7 November 1987
Second Division
Attendance: 19,583

MANCHESTER CITY:	HUDDERSFIELD TOWN:
Nixon	Cox
Gidman	Brown
Hinchcliffe	Bray
Clements	Webster
Lake	Walford
Redmond	Barham
White	May
McNab	Shearer
Stewart	Winter
Adcock	Cork
Simpson	Banks

FOOTBALL IS full of ironies and sometimes the least appealing games on paper can prove the most fascinating. This game proved to be a case in point with apparently little to entice the die-hards into Maine Road on a dull late autumn Manchester afternoon.

Like Alan Partridge on the Norwich ring road, City were going nowhere and, frankly, times were hard financially and there was little sign that things would improve anytime soon.

The 19,000 or so City fans in the ground that day has, over the course of time, become more like 50,000 – if the amount of people claiming to have been present is to be believed.

The truth is, there were plenty of people who had better things to do and didn't fancy a mundane-looking clash with bottom-of-the-table Huddersfield Town.

The football had been so-so and the Blues had failed to win their previous three home games but had shown flashes of promise on the road where leaders Bradford City had been put to the sword 4-2 and Swindon had also conceded four on their own ground, going down 4-3.

There was a sense that, if all the stars aligned, Mel Machin's side could really go to town on someone, but it was a big if at that point.

Former Arsenal and Newcastle United legend Malcolm Macdonald was the new boss of Huddersfield Town and his side ran out with high hopes of adding to City's underwhelming start to the season.

Relegated from the top flight for the second time in four years, the previous May following relegation from the First Division, the Blues had managed just six wins out of 16 and sat uncomfortably in mid-table, unable to shake off the hangover of the previous campaign's inadequacies.

There was also the danger that City had become a side who were not good enough for the top flight but too good for the second tier – from such situations yo-yo clubs were born!

Huddersfield ran out in kit resembling a bruised banana, backed by a small but loud following that was perhaps 400 strong.

Macdonald had clearly fired his side up and the Terriers began by moving the ball around with confidence and looking dangerous almost every time they went forward.

In fact, it was only due to a combination of luck and poor finishing that the visitors weren't 3-0 up inside the first ten minutes, such was their dominance – Duncan Shearer missed all three chances, though that's being a tad harsh as he was just inches away on each occasion.

The football was crisp, incisive and belied their lowly position in the league. Had just one of those chances been converted, Huddersfield would probably have gone on and won the game but it wasn't going to be their day.

When City finally woke up, the axis quickly tipped in the hosts' direction. Paul Stewart's foray down the left flank created a god chance that was wasted by Paul Lake and then Tony Adcock, but after the danger was cleared for a throw, Neil McNab picked up the ball, drifted in from the left and then hit a low drive past Cox from 20 yards to put City 1-0 up after 13 minutes.

From thereon in, virtually everything City attempted ended up in the back of the net and the visitors' heads quickly dropped. Winger Paul Simpson was in fantastic form and as he began to see more and more of the ball, City's potency increased ten-fold. Suddenly the lethargic opening had been forgotten and when Tony Adcock poked through a pass to Stewart 16 minutes later, the former Blackpool striker made no mistake as he buried a low shot past Cox to double the lead.

Then Simpson overlapped Lake to whip in a cross that was thumped home by the head of Adcock on 34 minutes to make it 3-0 and it was Simpson again claiming an assist as he powered a low drive across the box for David White to prod home from a yard out. City were 4-0 up and cruising.

At half-time, former Huddersfield star Frank Worthington, the co-commentator to Martin Tyler for the day, suggested City could go on and reach double figures – but he didn't think that would actually happen.

His caution was understandable. It is often the case that when a side leads so convincingly at half-time, they tend to take their foot off the gas in the second period, but it didn't happen on this occasion.

Adcock added a fifth on 52 minutes and Stewart scored his second on 66. Within 60 seconds 6-0 had become 7-0 as Adcock became the first player to complete his treble and with 23 minutes still to go, ten was very much a possibility.

But it wasn't until the 80th minute – uncannily – that Stewart made it 8-0 and time was running out. Something unique was now possible and the opportunity to reach double figures now acted as an incentive to further punish Huddersfield. Step forward David White.

White made it 9-0 with five minutes left and the players knew they were actively part of creating club history – nine was incredible but ten would be historic.

The excitement was at fever pitch, but the tenth goal of the game went to Huddersfield who scored in the 88th minute through former Blue Andy May's penalty. Cue wild, ironic celebrations from the visiting fans whose gallows humour was all-too familiar for City fans.

Was there still time to grab number ten? As a ball was lobbed up front it was flicked into White's path and he was clear. With his electric pace he raced toward goal, rounded the keeper and planted the ball in the net.

Maine Road went crazy and then the final whistle blew seconds later. Malcolm Macdonald was almost too shell-shocked to speak afterwards, but he would have the last laugh as – typically – Huddersfield won the return 1-0.

Only City!

v Tottenham Hotspur 4-1

9 December 1967
First Division
Attendance: 35,792

MANCHESTER CITY:	TOTTENHAM HOTSPUR:
Mulhearn	Jennings
Book	Kinnear
Pardoe	Knowles
Doyle	Mullery
Heslop	Hay
Oakes	Mackay
Lee	Saul
Bell	Greaves
Summerbee	Gilzean
Young	Venables
Coleman	Jones

HAD THE weather been a few degrees warmer, or a couple of other games survived, this match would have been written about in print but never seen by the general public. The *Match of the Day* cameras had been elsewhere and as the big freeze continued, they hurriedly searched around for a game that was still likely to be on.

Six matches had been called off in the First Division as everything south of Stoke was buried under several inches of snow. The north-west had been affected, but not as badly and under the snow-covered pitches, the ground was firm but playable.

The pitch at Maine Road was a typical example; playable but covered in snow. The lines were marked in blue and cleared as much as they could be but if the expected drop in temperatures hit Moss Side as soon as the sun went down, there was every chance the game between City and Tottenham may not actually make it to the 90th minute. Nonetheless, the referee passed the game fit for purpose.

The Blues went into the match in third spot, trailing Manchester United by three points. Spurs were in fifth and knew a win at Maine Road could propel them into joint second, so there was everything to play for.

With ten goals in the previous two home league games, City were starting to click into top gear as the festive period approached. Spurs, meanwhile, had won four of their nine away games, losing the other five, so the smart money was on a home victory, but clearly, the visitors were dangerous if they were anywhere near their best.

As the kick-off approached, City went out to warm up on the pitch and test out the conditions – Tottenham elected to warm up in the dressing room and so had no idea how the pitch would play.

The Blues found themselves slipping as they knocked the ball about and as they returned to the dressing room, skipper Tony Book came up with the novel idea of removing the studs from his boots to leave a small screw bottom exposed – just enough to provide vital grip in the snow and ice.

His team-mates followed suit and already the Blues had a sizeable advantage over the north Londoners.

City's performance against Spurs on that wintry, snow-covered Maine Road pitch back in 1967 epitomised all that was great about Joe Mercer's all-conquering side. The Blues were irrepressible and made a mockery of the conditions with a display of grace, skill and attacking football at its very best. This game would go down in club folklore and warm the shivering souls on the treacherous terraces as more than 35,000 City fans were treated to an unforgettable 90 minutes.

This was a talented Tottenham side, too, with four future managers in their team in the shape of Joe Kinnear, Terry Venables, Dave Mackay and Alan Mullery – and it was the visitors who drew first blood with the lethal Jimmy Greaves putting Spurs ahead on seven minutes.

The prolific striker followed a Venables free kick from the edge of the box and with his poacher's instinct, found himself on the edge of the six-yard box with the ball at his feet, from where he then comfortably placed the ball past Ken Mulhearn for a surprise lead. City, however, were in no mood to roll over.

With the snow falling heavily, the Blues launched an attack featuring Mike Doyle, Franny Lee and Tony Coleman. Coleman's cross caused a goalmouth scramble and Mullery deflected the ball to Colin Bell who smashed the ball home from 18 yards out for a deserved equaliser.

Shortly after, Mike Summerbee sent in a cross to the edge of the box and Neil Young's stinging volley was well saved by a young Pat Jennings, the last real action of note in an entertaining first half.

Top scorer Young, having a superb game, must have thought he wasn't destined to get on the score sheet when he sent another shot crashing in from 30 yards out. This time, the ball smacked the bar and bounced to safety.

Young then found Summerbee with a perfect cross and the right-winger rose between two defenders to head the ball past Jennings and put the Blues ahead for the first time in the match.

From that point on, Spurs never stood a chance. With City in majestic flow, the visitors had no answer to constant waves of attacks.

In the 64th minute, the Blues increased their lead with a move that started with keeper Mulhearn and never once touched a Spurs player. Book found Lee who fed the ball to Summerbee just inside the Tottenham half. Lee scampered down the flank to receive Summerbee's clever return ball and whipped a wicked cross-shot that hit the foot of the post.

The enigmatic Coleman was following up and was presented with the easiest of chances to volley the ball into the back of the net and virtually seal the points.

Dispirited Spurs fell yet further adrift when Bell's shot was parried by Jennings and the ball fell to Young who finally scored the goal his all-round play richly deserved.

Both Young and Coleman hit the post with successive shots as the Blues attempted to pile the misery on for Tottenham but there was to be no more scoring.

The ballet on ice was over and the secret of City's sure-footedness was later revealed by skipper Book who advised his team-mates to unscrew their studs to leave just the tips of a metal thread showing, effectively making the boots perfect to grip the ice and snow.

That proved to be the difference on the day and as the Londoners skidded, slipped and tumbled, City played the ball around as though there wasn't a snowflake in sight.

v Ipswich Town **1-0**

11 April 1981
FA Cup semi-final, at Villa Park
Attendance: 46,537

MANCHESTER CITY:	**IPSWICH TOWN:**
Corrigan	Cooper
Ranson	Mills
McDonald	Butcher
Reid	Thijssen
Power	Osman
Caton	Beattie
Bennett	Wark
Gow	Muhren
Mackenzie	Mariner
Hutchison	Brazil
Reeves	Gates

I N SIMPLE terms, City were virtually written off before they even stepped out on to the pitch at Villa Park to face Bobby Robson's title-chasing Ipswich Town. The Suffolk side were going head-to-head with Aston Villa at the top of the First Division and had a side packed with quality who were also hoping to write their name into club folklore by achieving the domestic football Holy Grail – the league and FA Cup double.

City had hauled themselves away from the foot of the table after being rooted to the bottom until mid-October when John Bond took over from the sacked Tony Book and Malcolm Allison.

Bond had already steered City to within a whisker of a League Cup Final (only to be controversially denied by Liverpool over a two-legged semi-final) and the league form had been that of title contenders, so while on paper the odds were stacked with the Tractor Boys, in reality, the Blues were a threat. The prize was a place in the 100th FA Cup Final with the winners facing either Wolverhampton Wanderers or Tottenham Hotspur who were playing their semi at Hillsborough.

The dramatic FA Cup semi-final victory over Ipswich is still a favourite game for many City supporters who were there on the day. In fact, most prefer the memory of the fantastic win at Villa Park to the final itself, but given the result of the final, that's hardly surprising.

It was an amazing day for the Blues, but it could have been very different had Ipswich taken any of the early opportunities presented to them.

With half of the Holte End full of City fans and half full of Ipswich, the game kicked off at 3pm on an overcast Saturday – back when semi-finals used to be played on Saturday afternoons – and the East Anglians were soon on the attack.

Bobby Robson's Ipswich side was packed with quality, grace, talent ... and Alan Brazil – and they were riding high in the First Division table while John Bond's team had recovered from being relegation favourites to a comfortable mid-table position with formidable cup form.

The Suffolk outfit had eight full internationals – four English, two Dutch and two Scottish – compared to City's lone England man Joe Corrigan.

Current form for both sides suggested a tight encounter, but City struggled in the early minutes and the graceful Arnold Muhren presented Brazil with a sitter on 11 minutes but he contrived to miss the ball completely. Shame!

Tommy Hutchison then cleared a thunderous Kevin Beattie header off the line four minutes later as the Blues, playing in red and black stripes, grimly hung on.

City began to battle back inspired by Gerry Gow who informed Franz Thijssen of his presence with a crunching challenge that earned him a talking-to by referee Pat Partridge.

Eric Gates, he of the toothless grin, blasted the ball over from close range as Ipswich continued to spurn chances. Dave Bennett was scythed down by Beattie towards the break and Gow's vicious drive was gathered at the second attempt by future City keeper Paul Cooper.

The teams went into the break locked at 0-0 with the Blues slowly beginning to ask a few questions themselves and it was the three musketeers – Gow, Hutchison and McDonald – who were causing Town most problems.

Brazil missed yet another golden opportunity after the break and the dangerous Beattie, a constant threat from set pieces, almost put his side ahead on the hour with a header that went inches past the post.

The City defence were responding magnificently to the pressure with Tommy Caton in particular in outstanding form.

Beattie again sent a header inches over and the burly Ipswich defender must have guessed by that point it wasn't going to be their day.

A mid-air collision between Beattie and Bennett, minutes from time, saw the Ipswich man limp off and McCall come on as a replacement as tiredness began to take over. The referee finally blew for the end of 90 minutes and both teams took a much-needed breather before the extra time began.

City attacked the Holte End for the first period and with exactly 100 minutes on the clock, were awarded a free kick on the edge of the Ipswich box.

Skipper Paul Power, who had scored in every round but one, sized up the defensive wall and Steve Mackenzie rolled the ball gently into his path. The crowd held its breath as he whipped a curling shot towards the goal. Cooper scrambled across to his right as the ball sailed into the top left-hand corner of the net. Half the ground erupted and the blue masses behind the goal went wild.

City were on their way to the FA Cup Final for the first time since 1969 with a wonderful goal scored in the 100th minute which looked to be sending them to Wembley for the 100th final. Surely fate was playing a hand in the competition … or was it?

The celebrations continued for several minutes, but there were still 20 minutes to play. Yet there was a feeling that the game was as good as over. Flags, scarves and banners were raised as the City fans saluted their heroes and despite a few close calls, Ipswich looked totally demoralised and the scenes and noise that greeted the final whistle will live long in the memory of those who were there.

City supporters may not have had too many chances to celebrate over the past 30 years, but when they do, they party with the best of them.

As it turned out, it wasn't City's year after all. Despite being ahead in the final and the subsequent replay, it was Spurs who lifted the trophy in the Centenary Cup Final, not the Blues.

v Athletic Bilbao 3-3

17 September 1969
European Cup Winners' Cup, first round first leg
Attendance: 45,000

MANCHESTER CITY:	ATHLETIC BILBAO:
Corrigan	Iribar
Book	Saez
Pardoe	Aranguren
Doyle	Igartua
Booth	Echeberria
Oakes	Larrauri
Summerbee	Argoitia
Bell	Uriarte
Young	Arieta (sub Ortuondo 67)
Lee	Clemente (sub Estefano 630
Bowyer	Rojo

HAVING BEEN unceremoniously dumped out of the European Cup in the first round the previous season, City approached their next foray into continental competition with a far more relaxed, almost gung-ho attitude, concentrating on their attacking strengths instead of locking defensive horns with their opponents and ultimately paying a heavy price.

The Blues had been drawn away for the first leg and came into the match on the back of a stunning 3-0 win away to Tottenham Hotspur in the league. But things didn't go too smoothly for Joe Mercer's men – and this was even before they left Manchester Airport. The first problem was an infuriating five-hour delay as the plane, a Comet jet, was withdrawn from service with technical problems. The relief plane from London then had to have its wheels changed after the captain decided they were unfit for further use.

To make matters worse, Tommy Booth became ill and was diagnosed with tonsillitis shortly before the flight, making him doubtful for the game.

The team finally made the journey to Spain but on arrival, the coach sent to collect them sent Malcolm Allison into a rage. The vehicle was filthy and someone had been sick on one of the seats.

The Blues arrived at their hotel, checked in and then prepared for a training session some eight miles away. The coach driver that had taken them to the hotel refused to drive them anywhere else and another bus had to be ordered, but that was in an even worse condition.

Allison ordered a fleet of taxis instead and raged, 'I had heard of these sort of tactics before in Europe but I never really expected it to happen here. But then perhaps I should have known after the way Joe Mercer and myself were treated when we went to watch Bilbao in San Sebastian recently.

'We were given seats for the match behind a goal with a great pillar in our way. I was determined not to put up with that for there were plenty of seats available in the main stand. But even then it was only because officials of Zagreb, Bilbao's opponents' gave up their seats for us that we were able to get a decent view of the game.

'At the time I thought nothing of that, but now after the latest incident I know better. But I can assure you we will get our own back tonight.'

Mercer was his usual calm self as his side prepared for the game. He refused to allow the dirty tricks to upset his plans and said, 'We'll tackle the Spaniards in the same way we took Spurs on their own ground – and you know what happened there.'

The Blues had crushed Tottenham by playing a skilful brand of defensive football in their opponents' half and Mercer was delighted with the way his side had performed.

'I have maintained in the past that we needed to be tighter at the back, but I didn't mean we were going to stick nine or ten men in front of the goalkeeper,' said Mercer. 'Any fool can build a defensive wall like that provided the players are stupid enough to stand for it.

'The way I look at it is that if you are going to build a wall at all, build it on the halfway line. As soon as you lose the ball you are playing defensive football because then you have to get it back.'

With the City side pumped up and ready to exact their own brand of revenge, the Spaniards began systematically taking the Blues apart from the off and it looked as though there may be a mountain to climb in the return at Maine Road. Joe Corrigan, a young and relatively inexperienced goalkeeper at the time, seemed to let the atmosphere get the better of him and he looked nervous and edgy throughout the game. Booth, who had been passed fit, was slowed by a nasty knock to his ankle and was given the run-around by home forward Arieta.

Bilbao's incessant pressure paid off when, after just nine minutes, Agioitia made it 1-0. City were still punch-drunk when Clemente made it 2-0 not long after, but they refused to buckle and where many sides would have been engulfed by the slick Spaniards, the Blues dug in and started to play their game.

All was not lost and with the hosts unable to maintain the frenetic pace, City clawed a goal back just before half-time through Neil Young who rifled a typically powerful drive past Iribar.

Bilbao weren't finished and just when it seemed they were flagging slightly, they found their second wind and increased the lead to 3-1 with a goal from Uriarte.

To their credit, City, who had the bit between their teeth, continued to concentrate on knocking the ball around and sticking to their game-plan and were rewarded when walking-wounded Booth pulled another goal back with a header from a corner to make it 3-2 – a result that most sides would have settled for considering the way things had been going earlier in the match.

This, however, was no ordinary side and with five minutes left, Colin Bell drove forward onto a Tony Book pass, whipped in a low cross and the ball was turned past Iribar by Bilbao defender Echeverri for a dramatic equaliser.

The City fans celebrated and it was no more than Mercer's courageous side deserved – it was the result the players needed to give them the belief to progress in the competition.

'The lads are not satisfied. They were a bit niggled at the end because they thought they could have won. But just wait until we play the second leg. We'll play aggressively and really give Bilbao something to think about,' said Allison later.

The Blues were true to his word and won the return at Maine Road 3-0 in front of almost 50,000 fans with goals from Ian Bowyer, Bell and Alan Oakes.

With confidence flying high, City went all the way to the final and beat Gornik Zabrze 2-1 in Vienna. Few doubted the path had been cleared by the magnificent comeback in Bilbao.

v Manchester United 5-1

23 September 1989
First Division
Attendance: 43,246

MANCHESTER CITY:	MANCHESTER UNITED:
Cooper	Leighton
Fleming	Anderson
Hinchcliffe	Donaghy
Bishop	Duxbury
Gayle	Phelan
Redmond	Pallister
White	Beardsmore (Sharpe)
Morley	Ince
Oldfield	McCalir
Brightwell	Hughes
Lake	Wallace

THIS WAS an afternoon no City fan will ever forget. It was a day when everything went right on the pitch but there would also be a huge price to pay for all the celebrations and taunting by the buoyant Blues faithful – it was to be the last derby win over United in 13 years prior to the last-ever Maine Road derby in 2002.

Still, if you are only going to have one win in 13 years against your deadliest of rivals, it must be done in style and nobody could argue that the Blues did exactly that on a fairly mild September afternoon back in 1989.

City, just promoted and back among the nation's elite, began the 111th Manchester derby having won only one match of the new campaign. Four points from 18 represented an awful start for Mel Machin's men and United, though not setting the division on fire, had added multi-million pound signings such as Gary Pallister and Paul Ince to their squad and were clear favourites to take all three points.

By comparison, City's entire squad had cost around £2.5m, but did include six Manchester-born players. Alex Ferguson was relatively new to the Reds and this was his first Manchester derby. Both clubs lost influential players shortly before the kick-off with Neil McNab and Clive Allen missing for City while United's Bryan Robson failed a late fitness test.

Respected Bolton referee Neil Midgley blew for kick-off as the deafening noise of more than 43,000 supporters packed into Maine Road reached fever pitch.

It was matters off the pitch, however, that grabbed the crowd's attention early on when fighting broke out in the North Stand. Dozens of United supporters had infiltrated the seats reserved for home support only and the game was held up for eight minutes as police ejected the troublemakers, having terrorised areas usually filled with families and young kids.

The players re-emerged from the dressing room and re-started the game. It was City who seemed to have drawn impetus from the incident and ten minutes later, the Blues went ahead. David White dragged a cross back hopefully into the United box. Pallister was caught flat-footed, the ball rolled to David Oldfield and he buried a rising shot past Jim Leighton and into the roof of the net.

City fans barely had time to stop celebrating the first goal before they were once again dancing in the aisles.

Paul Lake scrambled towards the United goal and forced Leighton to parry his shot, but Trevor Morley was first to the loose ball with a brave lunge and toe-poked home the Blues' second goal in the space of a minute.

Maine Road went wild. The 2-0 scoreline didn't flatter the Blues either, and they quickly set about attempting to finish the game before half-time.

United couldn't respond and with only one Mancunian in their side, it seemed they didn't have the heart to save themselves.

Meanwhile, City poured forward relentlessly. Steve Redmond won the ball in his own half and fed Oldfield down the right-hand flank. Roared on by the Kippax, the former Luton man drove forward and whipped in a perfect cross for new cult hero Ian Bishop to plant the ball past Leighton with a magnificent diving header.

The game was as good as over with just 36 minutes on the clock and the City fans were in dreamland. United looked bewildered and beaten and the half-time whistle was something of a disappointment for the home fans who wanted the game to continue for as long as possible.

A display as perfect as the first 45 could only be hindered by a break and for a while, that was exactly how the second half panned out.

United had more purpose and invention about their play and after 51 minutes, finally pulled a goal back. Russell Beardsmore crossed for future City boss Mark Hughes to volley a typically spectacular and unstoppable drive past Paul Cooper.

Danny Wallace then had a fine run and shot minutes later as the game went from joyous to torturous in the space of a few minutes for the Blues fans.

But this was City's day and as if re-awakened, Machin's side stormed back. Lake again found his way through the visitors' defence and had a shot saved before squaring the rebound to Oldfield who tapped the ball into an empty net for his second and City's fourth.

With a 4-1 deficit, United's hopes of a revival were again in shreds and four minutes later, unbridled joy became ecstasy for City with perhaps one of the best derby goals of all time.

The irrepressible Bishop fed White with a measured ball and White crossed first time for Andy Hinchcliffe to power a bullet header past a forlorn Leighton to end the contest with just over an hour gone.

The Kippax taunted Ferguson and the United fans who tried to leave – only to be rebuffed by stewards – all with just 62 minutes played! The Blues took pity on the Reds and, somehow, 5-1 remained the final score, though nobody was complaining.

City boss Machin said later, 'I was proud of my players. Proud of the way they approached the game and proud of the way they conducted themselves in achieving this splendid result.

'I thought we'd reached a standard of perfection in the 10-1 demolition of Huddersfield Town a couple of seasons back, but this latest performance surpassed even that and it's left me with a lovely feeling.'

Sentiments echoed by each and every City fan, though just six weeks later, Machin was sacked after a 6-0 defeat at Derby County. Is there any other sport where fortunes can change so dramatically in such a short period of time?

15 v Leeds United 2-1

7 January 1978
FA Cup third round
Attendance: 38,516

MANCHESTER CITY:	LEEDS UNITED:
Corrigan	Harvey
Clements	Reaney (A Clarke)
Donachie	F Gray
Booth	Cherry
Watson	McQueen
Owen	Madeley
Barnes	Harris
Bell	Hankin
Kidd	Currie
Hartford	Flynn
Tueart	Graham

THE THIRD round FA Cup tie City played at Elland Road, Leeds, in January 1978 was not only a classic of its kind, but represents a microcosm of all that was 1970s football – two star-studded sides, flowing football, flowing hair, heaving terraces, ill discipline among the players and considerable crowd trouble.

Bill Elliot, writing in *The Express*, was moved to say, 'It takes a rare kind of match to overcome pitch invasions, 16 minutes of stoppage and some of the worst crowd behaviour in the history of our football. The fact that there was as much talk about the game on the park as the sickness on the terraces highlights just how special was Manchester City's defeat of Leeds United ...'

City's side, containing internationals in almost every position, was fresh from a glorious season where the Blues finished a single point behind the champions Liverpool. That 1976/77 campaign had also witnessed a great run to the fifth round of the FA Cup, where City were more than unfortunate to exit at Leeds, having ably disposed of Newcastle and West Brom, when Trevor Cherry's late toe-poke ended hopes for another year – a year, in fact, when many had felt it was City's turn to lift the famous old trophy.

Here then – just under a year later – was an opportunity for the Blues to exact revenge on the Yorkshiremen.

A packed Elland Road witnessed a flowing classic of a match from the very first whistle. With Peter Barnes and Dennis Tueart swapping wings throughout the first half, City took the game to a heavily fancied Leeds side, who had already completed the league double over Tony Book's side by that point. Led by the inspirational Colin Bell, four games into his emotive comeback, Gary Owen and a typical never-say-die performance from Asa Hartford, City were firing on all cylinders in the middle of the park.

The first half saw the Leeds rearguard endure spells of heavy pressure with Tueart heading just wide after great work on the right by Owen and Barnes's jinking run ending with McQueen upending him for a nailed-on penalty that the referee decided against giving.

Such was the visitors' dominance, by the end of the first 45 the Leeds players had taken to fighting among themselves.

After a series of City corners threatened to create havoc, David Harvey and McQueen were spoken to by the referee after swinging wild punches at each other. The referee even saw fit to walk to the touchline and warn Leeds manager Jimmy Armfield to get his team under control.

This would be a prelude to more serious problems later in the game, as some of the Leeds supporters, buoyed by what they had seen on the pitch, would decide to ape (an apt word on this occasion) their heroes' unprofessional behaviour.

Somehow, however, Leeds survived the onslaught to retreat to the shelter of the changing rooms at 0-0.

City's attacks did not let up after the interval and, after McQueen had fouled Brian Kidd on 62 minutes, they got the richly deserved breakthrough.

With the City fans packing the terraces behind the goal and all the way down the side of the ground as far as the halfway line, there was a huge upswell of noise as Watson lofted the ball forward, Bell bravely looped the ball on with his head and Tueart flung himself through the bodies to head high past Harvey.

As the net bulged, Tueart was treated to a mouthful of turf as Paul Reaney arrived too late and squashed him into the penalty area mud.

A mass of sky blue scarves greeted the goal, but City were not finished. Leeds, committed now to chasing the equaliser, were leaving gaps at the back, as the game ebbed and flowed furiously.

City's killer second goal came with 18 minutes to go, as Donachie crossed from the left wing, Bell got up above Frank Gray to head powerfully forward, Harvey – mis-timing his jump slightly – pushed the ball up on to the bar and, as players rushed in on the loose ball, Barnes got a toe end to it and it was in the back of the net, doubling the Blues' lead.

Clarke's rugged challenge on Joe Corrigan just after this earned him a talking-to from the referee as the atmosphere on the Leeds Kop began to change palpably for the worse.

Sure enough, with 13 minutes left on the clock, a massive surge of Leeds fans carried those at the front on to the pitch at the Kop end.

With City dominating the home team, this was the home fans' solution – try and get the game abandoned. Referee Seal took the teams off and, to his credit, re-appeared with a tiny microphone to tell the supporters, 'This match will not be abandoned.'

He repeated his mantra for effect (earning great cheers from the travelling City fans) before the players finally re-appeared some 15 minutes later.

By now, the game had lost its pattern, the crowd were being held back by police horses and most wanted it to finish as quickly as possible.

City continued to press. Tueart had a great chance on the breakaway to make it 3-0, but it was Tony Currie who was bossing things now and he it was who inspired Leeds' mini comeback, being upended by Corrigan in the box at the end of a weaving run. The penalty was despatched low to Corrigan's left by Frank Gray, to create a tense finale.

With the thousands of Blues fans singing their songs of victory, the whistle finally went with the clock past 5pm to end an epic day of cup football.

The draw for the fourth round was unkind in the extreme – after the valiant effort of beating Leeds on their own turf, City were drawn away to Brian Clough's all-conquering Nottingham Forest and eventually went out 2-1. The memories of the battling and swashbuckling display in Yorkshire would not be dimmed, however.

v Stoke City 3-1

5 September 1981
First Division
Attendance: 25,256

MANCHESTER CITY:	STOKE CITY:
Corrigan	Fox
Ranson	Evans
McDonald	Hampton
Reid	Dodd
Caton	O'Callaghan
Power	Doyle
O'Neill	Griffiths
Gow	Heath
Hartford	Chapman
Francis	Bracewell
Reeves	Maguire (Ursem)

WHEN TREVOR Francis walked onto the sun-lit Victoria Ground pitch at Stoke at 3pm on 5 September 1981, he carried the high hopes of the blue half of Manchester on his not-too-broad shoulders.

When he walked off it at the end of a tumultuous match, he said, 'I'll never forget my £1m debut for Nottingham Forest at Ipswich. After 30 minutes the fans were singing "what a waste of money"! I didn't give them the same opportunity this time!'

After a long struggle to find a decent striker, John Bond had finally managed to beat Ron Atkinson to the coveted Forest man's signature and make him the first player ever to cost £1m twice.

United had wanted to trade former Forest striker Garry Birtles for Francis, but that idea had been kiboshed by Brian Clough, owing to the fact that Birtles's flow of goals at Old Trafford had never breached the level of a parched trickle.

City had started the season well enough with a 2-1 home win over West Brom, but it had been the midweek draw at lowly Notts County which concerned Bond who believed the Blues had not got enough firepower up front to take the team on from the previous May's FA Cup Final defeat to Spurs.

Francis was spotted in the stands at Meadow Lane that night and Bond raised the stakes in the after-match press conference by saying, 'After tonight's game, I'm moving in even stronger for Trevor.'

Assistant John Benson added, 'If we had had Trevor in the side tonight, we would have won it by half-time.'

The travelling City faithful – more than 10,000 had gathered in the away end at the Victoria Ground after something akin to Francis hysteria broke out – were in good spirits but even the most optimistic among them couldn't have guessed that Francis was about to explode into our consciousness with a debut that would only be matched sporadically thereafter. With Peter Fox performing heroics from the beginning, Stoke, starting the game as surprise early leaders of the division, were under intense pressure.

They held out until the 35th minute when Bobby McDonald's long clearance found new-boy Francis running free in a promising position.

He proceeded to turn the gangly Brendan O'Callaghan inside out before moving inside Ray Evans and again meeting O'Callaghan tracking back as best he could. Rounding the defender for a second time, he hit a low shot through Fox's legs to the delight of the Blues fans behind the goal.

Stoke battled back after the break and Chapman equalised after an hour, running towards Corrigan with Tommy Caton in hot pursuit and sliding the ball past City's giant keeper.

City moved Phil Boyer into the injured Paul Power's midfield slot and the battle raged again. Within five minutes the Blues had regained the lead as Gerry Gow put Francis away down the right. His centre got stuck in a group of bodies and Kevin Reeves eventually prodded home with ex-City stalwart Mike Doyle helpless to intervene.

By the time Francis had wrapped the game up with his second and City's third, the fans were comparing his debut favourably with those of Denis Law, Colin Bell and Dennis Tueart before him.

Francis had only had lunchtime to acclimatise to his new surroundings (John Bond had famously brought the new signing into the hotel where City's players were having lunch and said, somewhat unnecessarily, 'This is Trevor, he's here to give us the confidence to win things.').

Afterwards the press pack was eating out of the striker's hand. Although his magic would rub off on the rest of the team, Francis would only play one injury-ravaged season for City, before being sold to Italian Serie A outfit Sampdoria to lessen the terrible financial burden being carried by the club at the time. He would later be quoted on the subject of Peter Swales's profligacy that the former City chairman was a man who went out to buy a Jaguar and came back with a Rolls. Francis's self-image was never low, that can be confidently said!

Bond's dream of domination would turn to ashes the following season when he resigned after a shambolic cup defeat at Brighton. With Francis's unforgettable debut fading to the back of Blues fans' minds, City went down to the Second Division just a year and a half after his sunshine debut in the Potteries.

In later years, Francis would recall his debut with great affection: 'I was very surprised by the number of City supporters who had travelled to Stoke to watch my debut – 12,000 I'm told – and to this day, whenever I cover City matches in my capacity as commentator for Sky Sports, I always bump into someone who happened to be at that game – it seems that every Man City fan was at that game and that's all people ever want to talk about.

'As an example, one of my great passions in life is music and I was in London near Marylebone when I bumped into Noel Gallagher who I'd never met before – all I wanted to talk about was music and his career but all he wanted to do was talk about my City debut at Stoke! I was quite chuffed in all honesty!

'I was only at Maine Road for a short period – much shorter than I would have liked – but I look back on that period with great affection. As surprised as I was to have left Forest, I was equally surprised to leave City after just one year, too – or a bit less than that, even.

'I'd set off for the World Cup in 1982 with England and wasn't aware that I was being watched by Sampdoria.

'I went on holiday after we'd gone out of the competition and had no idea what was happening behind the scenes or that I was about to be invited to Italy for a possible transfer which eventually went through.

'I was really happy at City because the club had such fantastic supporters who I loved playing in front of. I didn't have an injury-free season and missed a lot of games, but I think my record of 14 goals in 29 games stands up pretty well and like to think I was good value during my time there.'

v Juventus 1-0

15 September 1976
UEFA Cup first round first leg
Attendance: 36,955

MANCHESTER CITY:	JUVENTUS:
Corrigan	Zoff
Docherty	Cuccureddu
Donachie	Gentile
Doyle	Furino
Watson	Morini
Conway	Scirea
Barnes (Power)	Causio
Kidd	Tardelli
Royle	Marchetti
Hartford	Benetti
Tueart	Bettega

CITY'S 'REWARD' for winning the League Cup Final 2-1 against Newcastle United seven months before was drawing one of the pre-tournament favourites Juventus in the opening round of the UEFA Cup.

The Blues had returned to Europe after an absence of four years for the start of the 1976/77 season where they faced the Turin giants who, although being one of the grandest names in world football and the most successful Italian team of the 20th century, were, surprisingly, still without a European trophy having lost the European Cup Final in 1973.

They had also lost against three of the four English clubs they had previously met in Europe, going out to Leeds United, Liverpool and Wolverhampton Wanderers but edging through against Derby County.

It was very much a monkey on the back of the Old Lady and one that had cost a succession of managers their position. It was time to deliver and the players knew it, but if Juventus were focused on silverware, so were Tony Book's City who were unbeaten in their first five league games that season and were looking to make a serious challenge for the First Division title.

As a gauge of how strong the Serie A outfit were at this point, it's worth noting that many of the Juventus side that faced City in this tie went on to form the backbone of Italy's 1982 World Cup-winning side.

Goalkeeping legend Dino Zoff, Antonio Cabrini and Claudio Gentile made a formidable defensive trio while Marco Tardelli graced their midfield. Their manager Giovanni Trapattoni would later become Italy's World Cup boss for Japan/Korea 2002 and was in charge of the Republic of Ireland between 2008 and 2013.

The general feeling prior to this match was that the Blues would need a minimum two-goal lead to take to Turin because anything else against a team renowned for getting the job done on their own patch would likely see Book's side exit the competition at a disappointingly early stage.

The Blues had done their homework, but everything would hinge on the ability to take their chances – and with Juventus's defensive strength measurable against any side in Europe, that meant their opportunities were likely to be few and far between.

Juventus allowed City plenty of possession on the night and were quite happy to try and hit the Blues on the break. On the occasions City did penetrate the Italians' back four, international Zoff showed why he was perhaps the best in the world at the time by producing two world-class saves – one in particular, from Brian Kidd, was not dissimilar to Gordon Banks's wondrous one-handed stop against Pele in 1970.

He also somehow tipped a Dennis Tueart effort onto the crossbar as City gave it their all, but the longer the Italians resisted, the more the tie tipped in their favour.

Tueart, Brian Kidd, Peter Barnes and Joe Royle caused the visitors headaches all night in what was proving a bruising affair.

Then, with seconds of the first half remaining, a breakthrough came after 44 minutes as former Manchester United and Arsenal striker Kidd wrestled a yard of space to plant a firm header down to the left of Zoff following Tueart's corner and Royle's flick-on. The keeper had no chance. The near 37,000 Maine Road crowd erupted and it was no more than City deserved – plus the timing couldn't have been better.

Suddenly, the Italians' mask slipped and the visitors resorted to some cynical challenges aimed at stopping the Blues increasing their advantage.

Barnes, always a threat, limped out of the game on the hour after several crunching tackles that would have earned straight red cards each time in today's game. There was shirt-pulling, sly digs and feigning injury.

The Blues needed to keep their cool and in Asa Hartford, they had the perfect midfield general to hold things together. The Scotland international was outstanding and had the injured Colin Bell been available, City might well have put the game out of Juventus's reach as they continued to knock on the door throughout the second half, but the elusive second goal wouldn't come.

At the final whistle, the Italians congratulated each other, knowing that a 1-0 defeat was, in effect, a moral victory and that the return leg would be an entirely different affair.

After the game, a confident Book boldly stated, 'I don't say we will win in Italy, but we will do enough to qualify for the next round.'

Memories of Malcolm Allison's 'we'll terrify Europe' statement flooded back.

As it turned out, the general fear that one goal wasn't going to be enough was confirmed in the second leg in Turin.

Though the Blues' rearguard held out well under intense pressure, defender Gaetano Scirea put the hosts level on aggregate on 38 minutes and with 55,000 Italians roaring on Trapattoni's men, it seemed just a matter of time before the second goal came and, when Roberto Boninsegna doubled the advantage on 69 minutes, the tie was as good as over.

Juventus promptly shut up shop, kept possession and ran the clock down until the final whistle. The Turin side then completed a Manchester double, beating United in the second round 3-0 in the return leg having lost the first leg at Old Trafford 1-0.

They saw off Shakhtar Donetsk 3-1 on aggregate in the third round before eliminating FC Magdeburg, AEK Athens and, finally, winning the competition by beating Athletic Bilbao on the away goals rule after a two-legged final.

Their wait for European glory was finally over, but no team had pushed them quite as hard as City had and the Blues would come within a whisker of winning the league title later that season, ultimately being trumped by Liverpool by a single point.

v Everton 2-2

7 March 1981
FA Cup quarter-final
Attendance: 52,791

MANCHESTER CITY:	EVERTON:
Corrigan	McDonough
Ranson	Gidman
McDonald	Ratcliffe
Reid	Wright
Power	Lyons
Caton	Ross
Tueart	McMahon
Gow	Eastoe
Mackenzie	Varadi
Hutchison	Hartford
Reeves	O'Keefe (Stanley)

GOODISON PARK in 1981 was an intimidating place to visit and with thick grey clouds floating in on off the Irish Sea and nearly 53,000 fans packed in to see who would edge a step closer to Wembley, it was perhaps more hostile than ever.

City, backed by more than 10,000 travelling fans, had been resurrected under John Bond's flamboyant leadership and had swept through the early rounds of the FA Cup.

They dished out a 4-0 thrashing to Malcolm Allison's Crystal Palace and then comprehensively saw off the club Bond had left for City – Norwich – beating the Canaries 6-0, before edging into the last eight by beating Fourth Division Peterborough United at London Road in the fifth round thanks to Tommy Booth's solitary goal.

This then was to be a battle royal with Gordon Lee's Everton with the reward a place in the last four of England's most prestigious competition – a prospect which would have made Blues fans laugh out loud in October when City were cast adrift at the bottom of the table, headed for relegation and in complete disarray on and off the pitch.

With the noise deafening and City backed by their huge contingent of travelling fans, the two sides went hammer and tongs at each other in a style that only the FA Cup can seemingly inspire.

Everton were lining up with four players who would play for City in future years in the shape of Steve McMahon, Imre Varadi and John Gidman. The fourth, Asa Hartford, had graced the Blues' midfield for several years during the 1970s and was a player always afforded a warm reception on his returns to Maine Road.

Today, however, there was no love lost. There was a new, gnarly Scot patrolling the City midfield now in the shape of Gerry Gow and the duel between him and Hartford was fascinating to watch.

With no quarter asked and none given, Hartford and Gow swapped bone-crunching tackles in midfield in the early stages as each side sought a foothold and it was left to Mackenzie and Power to try and make headway for City.

However, despite having some reasonable half-chances during an aggressive first half, City went behind just before the break as Peter Eastoe drew first blood for the home side, receiving the ball in the box before steadying himself enough to poke the ball past Joe Corrigan and send the home fans wild.

With the ground shuddering to the Everton fans' celebrations, City were back in it with a rapier thrust just two minutes later with half-time just moments away. Power's looping cross from the left was expertly headed down by Kevin Reeves into the path of the unmarked Gow, who, having escaped from Hartford's shackles for a moment, fired a superb rising shot into the top right-hand corner from six yards out.

The atmosphere was electric in what was turning into a typical blood and thunder English FA Cup tie.

Three minutes into the second half City were behind again though in somewhat controversial circumstances. As Eastoe passed for Varadi, the Everton striker seemed to have pushed the ball too far past Tommy Caton and as he passed the City centre-back he fell to the floor dramatically in front of the baying hordes on the Gwladys Street terrace.

Referee Peter Willis (an old foe of City's) had no doubts about the illegality of the challenge and pointed to the spot, despite City's protestations. Everton, having missed two penalties the week before, needed a cool head and they found one in Trevor Ross who made no mistake from the spot, putting the home side back in front at 2-1.

The effort that went into City's second fight back was breathtaking and bore testament to the belief Bond had driven into his team, who never seemed to know when they were beaten.

With time running out and the pitch cutting up into little more than a potato patch, the Blues surged forward time and again until, in the 84th minute, the Everton defence was finally breached once again.

A classic City build-up down the left saw two separate one-twos played between Reeves and Mackenzie and then Mackenzie and Power. Power, the epitome of that terrific cup run (he scored in every round bar the tie with Peterborough), dug deep to find the energy which carried him on to the edge of the box before scooping a tired right leg at the ball, just as Mick Lyons came thundering in with his challenge.

His lob sailed high over the out-rushing Jim McDonough and seemed to hang for an eternity before dropping underneath the crossbar and into the back of the net. The celebrations began behind the goal in the Park End terraces and Power was swamped by his team-mates.

At 2-2, the scoring was finished and the teams would have to meet again at Maine Road four days later. Both teams had given their all and were mentally and physically spent though it was the thousands of travelling Mancunians who travelled back up the East Lancs road the happiest, still feeling this could be the year.

The Sunday papers named it 'abrasive', 'supercharged', 'gruelling', 'livewire' and 'energy-sapping'. It had been all of that and much more.

Gripped by cup fever, 52,000 fans crammed into Maine Road for the replay and two goals in a minute from full-back Bobby McDonald, plus another from Power – his fourth goal of the cup run – sealed a memorable 3-1 win over the Toffees as City steamed into the semi-final where Bobby Robson's Ipswich Town awaited.

v West Ham United 4-3

21 October 1972
First Division
Attendance: 30,890

MANCHESTER CITY:	WEST HAM UNITED:
Healey	Grotier
Book	McDowall
Donachie	Lampard
Doyle	Bonds
Booth	taylor
Jeffries	Moore
Summerbee	Ayris
Bell	Best
Marsh	Holland
Lee	Brooking
Towers	Robson

AFTER FIVE years of rightly being considered as one of the nation's powerhouses, City went into this game with the spectre of an unlikely relegation battle ahead of them.

After the glorious era just a few years earlier, the Blues were beginning to struggle to live up to those trophy-laden seasons. City had finished the previous season fourth after being in sight of the title right up until the final days of the campaign, ultimately falling short by a point.

The Blues had started the new season erratically and even found themselves anchored to the bottom of the table in early September after a defeat to Crystal Palace at Selhurst Park.

The team was ageing and there were a number of new faces who weren't integrating particularly well with one era ending and another one beginning.

This was the first season without the steadying influence of Joe Mercer, who had been forced out during a boardroom takeover and was now to be found in charge of Coventry City, leaving Malcolm Allison with carte blanche to tinker with the team as he liked.

Big Mal had craved the chance to be his own man and felt he was more than just a coach – he wanted recognition as a manager and felt the time was right and fortunately for Mal, he had friends in high places, namely the boardroom where his admirers were legion.

A 40-year-old self-made millionaire, Peter Swales, who had made his fortune in radio and hi-fi retail, was the new chairman and a bright new era was supposedly beginning for the Blues with the old guard out and the new, younger regime in.

Yet on the pitch, things were rapidly going into decline. A 4-1 defeat to Birmingham City underlined the defensive frailties of Allison's Blues and this was followed by a 5-1 loss to second-bottom Stoke City in the next away match a fortnight later and already questions were being asked of Allison's ability to manage.

More embarrassingly, City slipped to their seventh successive away reverse of the campaign in the match prior to the visit of the Hammers as they went down 3-2 to Mercer's new Sky Blues at Highfield Road. Nobody could have complained if Mercer left the ground with a wry smile that day.

Four wins and a draw from six home games meant that, by mid-October, City were in the bottom three, just ahead of Manchester United who were also living on past reputation.

West Ham United were faring better in eighth place but their star-studded side was also beginning to disintegrate, although some, such as Billy Bonds, Bobby Moore and a young Trevor Brooking still remained.

Martin Peters and Geoff Hurst had already been sold on to Spurs and Stoke respectively by this time, but despite this, the Irons were giving a decent account of themselves, particularly at Upton Park where they'd dropped just one point. Like City, they too struggled on the road.

They were, however, still smarting from a shambolic League Cup exit at the hands of Fourth Division Stockport County and once again travelled north looking to put that disaster out of their minds. The 30,890 crowd that assembled that October day was not aware how close they came to seeing City perform without the man who turned out to be the match's catalyst.

Colin Bell had spent the whole of the previous week laid low with a stomach bug, but he hauled himself out of his sick bed not only to take part in the game, but to run the show completely from start to finish with a heroic display in what turned out to be an exhilarating match.

'I felt a bit hazy at times,' Bell admitted stoically to the press afterwards – though it hadn't showed as City tore into the East Londoners right from the start.

In their previous game the Blues had been criticised for a lack of cohesion at Coventry. The passes on this occasion, however, found their targets with unerring accuracy and City's football flowed magnificently as West Ham were swept away in a feast of attacking football that produced six first-half goals.

By half-time, City were 4-2 up, though the Hammers were still very much in the game with goals from Tony Towers, Mike Summerbee and two from Rodney Marsh interspersed by a couple from West Ham's Bermudian striker Clyde Best and Johnny Ayris.

Attack after attack stemmed from the gentle prompting of Bell as City ran rings around their guests. Showing no signs of the illness that had sidelined him, and ably assisted by the young Towers, Bell ran effortlessly from end to end in constant support of Marsh, Lee and Summerbee in City's attack.

Inevitably, the foot was taken off the accelerator in the second half and City conceded a third goal to England legend Moore, leaving an unnecessarily edgy finish for the faithful to endure.

This game would herald a terrific run in November, which saw City defeat Derby County, Manchester United and Everton with an aggregate score of 10-2 in consecutive games, to lift them well clear of trouble.

Their inconsistent form would continue to dog them throughout the campaign, however, and City finished in 11th position – a final placing the Blues would have taken without question.

The West Ham game would remain one of only a few really positive memories of that season and would typify the worth of Bell to the Blues, even when not fully fit but for Big Mal, the magic had faded and in March he decided it was time to move on and resigned from his post.

v Sunderland 3-2

11 May 1991
First Division
Attendance: 39,194

MANCHESTER CITY:	SUNDERLAND:
Margetson	Norman
Hill	Owers
Pointon	Hardyman (Brady)
Heath	Bennett
Hendry	Ord
Redmond	Pascoe
White	Bracewell
Brennan	Hawke (Hauser)
Quinn	Davenport
Harper	Gabbiadini
Clarke (Beckford)	Kay

FINISHING THE season with a game affecting the relegation places and having Luton Town involved in the dogfight are ingredients to make even the most hardened City supporter turn towards the drinks cabinet.

David Pleat and Raddy Antic still hold an unwelcome but steadfast place in City folklore, even after all these years.

However, on Saturday 11 May 1991, a funny thing happened. City entered the last weekend of the season with no relegation worries and found themselves intertwined in a plot that offered them an unusually nerveless cameo role.

It was Sunderland who arrived firmly under the relegation spotlight on this occasion with the Blues poised to wrap up a magnificent season under Peter Reid and Sam Ellis – the best in the league since 1978, in fact.

The achievement was all the more impressive taking into account that Reid had only taken on this first job at managerial level after Howard Kendall had jumped ship to Goodison Park the previous December, citing City as a love affair but Everton as a marriage. Whatever, Howard …

The Wearsiders arrived at Maine Road needing a win to take them above Luton – so long as the Hatters slipped up at home to Derby County, who City had relegated two weeks before in the famous 'Niall Quinn game', where he scored a goal and then replaced the sent-off Tony Coton in goal and saved a penalty from Dean Saunders.

This was the kind of afternoon made for City who were used to rollercoaster finishes to seasons and, in fact, expected nothing less. What could be worse than finishing the campaign with a boring, mid-table knock-around with nothing at stake?

Maine Road was heaving with the attendance just a fraction under 40,000. A huge 8,000-strong contingent from Sunderland filling the Platt Lane Stand added to the carnival atmosphere inside the ground.

Thankfully, the players didn't disappoint. In a pulsating first half, both sides netted twice to go in level 2-2 at the break.

Quinn, ending a fantastic campaign during which he had led the line with grace and goals, put City ahead after only ten minutes. Defender John Kay got in a mess from a long ball into Sunderland's box and the tall striker coolly slotted home.

It was almost half-time before Sunderland recovered, but they did so in style, Marco Gabbiadini heading in at the end of a sweeping move up the left, again involving Kay and then City old-boy Gary Bennett headed home after a huge scramble in the City box to make it 2-1 minutes later. Cue pandemonium in the visitors' end.

With the Sunderland hordes hanging on to the fencing at the front of the Platt Lane Stand the atmosphere was electric. The reporter at Luton then told those listening to their radios, 'If I tell you that Derby's Mick Harford has scored here …' Cue more celebrations as it appeared the Great Escape was on, but it would be a cruel joke as it transpired the bruising forward had in fact scored in his own net to put Luton one up!

Football can be a merciless game and worse was to follow as the Black Cats' support went from one end of the delirium scale to the other. As the atmosphere among the away fans shifted and the first period moved into injury time, Quinn burst onto a loose ball in the Sunderland area (this time the nervous Gary Owers kicking air instead of leather) and hammered a low shot past Norman to even the scores once more and send the teams in level at the break.

It seemed that the old ground would explode, such was the feverish celebrations from all corners. But there was an extra twist, an incentive that may have been lost in the general football world – but not inside Maine Road.

City had their own agenda to follow with the chance of ending the season ahead of Manchester United in the final First Division table – an all too rare treat – so there were no thoughts of sympathy towards their struggling opponents.

In the space of five minutes Sunderland had equalised, gone ahead, seen Luton score and then conceded one themselves. It was a bitter pill to swallow for the breathless Wearsiders, but typical of the never-say-die attitude that the City of Peter Reid's stewardship possessed.

Reid had started the game with Quinn, David White and Wayne Clarke up front, in an attempt to have the same effect as the fortnight before when City had knocked in five at Villa Park. Finishing fifth would be an achievement for a club without any notable silverware since 1976 and no top five finishes for 15 years.

Increasingly desperate, Sunderland, their top-flight status in dire straits, were unable to find a way through in the second period as they threw numbers forward at every opportunity. Both Gabbiadini and Davenport found their paths blocked by heroic keeping from City stand-in Martyn Margetson and, as time ticked by, it seemed obvious that relegation would be the only outcome.

And there was to be one final blow. A desperate last surge forward by City brought the reward the football played thoroughly deserved.

As the ball arrived at the feet of Adrian Heath wide on the right, he chipped a cross up to the far post, where the incoming David White advanced at speed to tuck the ball past Norman and collide with the post in the process to send Maine Road into a frenzy.

The home supporters knew the magnitude of the goal meant that, after 13 years of finishing below United in the table, White's goal took City to fifth in the table, one place above United for the first time in more than a decade. What a game and what an end to the season.

v Sheffield United 2-1

25 August 1923
First Division
Attendance: 56,993

MANCHESTER CITY:	SHEFFIELD UNITED:
Mitchell	Gough
Cookson	Milton
Fletcher	Cook
Hamill	Pantling
Woosnam	Waugh
Pringle	Green
Donaldson	Mercer
Roberts	Sampy
Johnson	Johnson
Barnes	Gillespie
Murphy	Tunstall

WITH PLANS to build a new home ground first revealed at the end of the 1922/23 season, work began clearing a suitable plot of land in Moss Side, Manchester.

Hyde Road could not be expanded any further plus a devastating fire had destroyed the Main Stand a couple of years before meaning a change of scenery was the only logical solution.

Two sites in Belle Vue had been mooted but the land available was nowhere near enough to match the grand plans of the club's owners. The decision to move from east Manchester to south Manchester didn't go down well with everyone and one director resigned and formed a breakaway club, Manchester Central FC.

Despite this, and despite the fact that the new home was nearly called Dog Kennel Lane, it was a proud day for City and their fans when the Blues walked out into their brand new Moss Side home for the first time in August 1923. The crowd of 56,993 was a new attendance record for the club who had left the far less grand and somewhat crumbling surroundings of Hyde Road a few months earlier.

The former home and its unique atmosphere had not been completely forgotten, though. The goal posts had been literally moved and several turnstiles were integrated at Maine Road while the old main stand roof was transported to Halifax Town's The Shay to keep the rain off an entirely new set of shivering souls.

The total cost of the new stadium is almost impossible to trace but various reports seem to suggest it was in the region of £150,000 – about £12m by today's standards and a small fortune for the era.

Designed by Manchester architect Charles Swain and built by Sir Robert McAlpine builders in less than 12 months, the whole ambitious project was a tribute to all concerned in both its design and construction.

Maine Road's capacity was more than double that of Hyde Road and was built to house approximately 80,000. Only Wembley Stadium, opened just months earlier, could hold more fans in England and the builders were in fact keen to make Maine Road 'the Wembley of the north'.

The vast bank of terracing facing the players as they ran out was known originally as the 'Popular Side' (later to become the Kippax Street Stand) and was where the main bulk of City fans gathered for the opening match – a trend that would continue until the ground's closure 80 years later).

With only the Main Stand roofed, much of the noise generated by the crowd was lost to the open air above their heads but there was still a tremendous atmosphere as Ernest Magnall's side took to the field of play.

Legendary all-round sportsman Max Woosnam was named as captain and it was he that led the Blues out as the assembled band played 'Ours Is a Nice House, Ours Is'.

Woosnam had missed the whole of the 1922/23 campaign with a leg fractured while colliding with a wooden fence at Hyde Road and also missed the chance to defend his Wimbledon doubles title during his absence – clearly not your average run of the mill footballer! No doubt immensely proud, the captain rallied the side to ensure the first game at Maine Road began with a victory – it was simple, there was no other choice.

The Lord Mayor of Manchester was then introduced to the players before ceremoniously kicking the match off then Tommy Johnson did it for real moments later on referee Howcroft's whistle, beginning a whole new, more financially viable era began for the Blues.

Sammy Cookson and Eli Fletcher, like Woosnam, had returned after lengthy lay-offs and Alec Donaldson, a recent signing from Bolton Wanderers, made his full league debut.

Manchester City's Greatest Games

Sheffield United were more than capable of ruining the day and had taken three out of the four points available in the previous season's corresponding fixtures and a number of Blades fans had crossed the Pennines to be part of this momentous occasion.

A tight first half ended without either side testing the new netting, despite Tommy Johnson and Horace Barnes forcing the visitors' keeper Gough into a couple of decent saves.

City came out for the second half determined to see off the South Yorkshire side's challenge and finally broke the deadlock almost halfway through the second period.

The prestigious honour of the first ever goal scored at Maine Road went to the prolific Barnes on 68 minutes after connecting with debutant Donaldson's cross to send the home fans into raptures. And there was even better to come as City tore into their opponents, buoyed by the vast crowd.

Strike partner Johnson made it 2-0 just three minutes later and the Blues could have really begun life with a Manchester 14 postcode in style when they were awarded a penalty and a chance to go 3-0 up shortly after as the visitors fell to pieces.

But, just as Barnes forever etched his name into the record books by scoring the first goal, Frank Roberts followed suit by becoming the first player to miss a penalty at the new ground despite the new introduction of the arc on the edge of the box which allowed the taker a good run-up to the spot.

Perhaps unnerved by the long run-up, Roberts hit his shot straight at Gough to give the visitors an unlikely lifeline.

The Blades, reduced to ten men through injury, duly scored in the 88th minute through Harry Johnson to ensure a tense finish – one of hundreds to follow at Maine Road over the years – but City held out for the victory the home crowd had demanded.

For skipper Woosnam it was to be his only league appearance of the season – no doubt his desire to lead out his team for such an historic occasion had clouded his judgement regarding the extent of his injury or rather he was determined to play at any cost.

His decision had not adversely affected the day's play and Maine Road was up and running with the best start possible.

v Stoke City **2-1**

29 December 1998
Second Division
Attendance: 30,478

MANCHESTER CITY:	STOKE CITY:
Weaver	Muggleton
Crooks	Small
Edghill	Woods
Wiekens	Sigurdsson
Vaughan	Petty
Horlock	Robinson
Brown	Kavanagh
Pollock	Oldfield
Taylor	Keen
Bishop (Goater 46)	Thorne
Dickov	Lightbourne (Sturridge 57)

OR ANY game in 1998 to qualify as one of Manchester City's greatest, the circumstances had to be special, unique or at least interesting.

With City at the lowest ebb in their history, wallowing in mid-table in their first ever season outside the top two divisions, something above the ordinary was required to kick-start a late bid for promotion.

It was either that or face the dreaded prospect of becoming a permanent addition to the lower leagues, Johnstone's Paint Trophy and potential banana skins in the FA Cup first and second rounds.

Boxing Day had suggested a slight stirring of the something with a soggy, rain-swept but most welcome 1-0 victory at Wrexham. That this had followed an embarrassing 2-1 defeat at York City and several other poor performances still did not bode well, but at least it perhaps suggested things had got as bad as they possibly could have at Bootham Crescent.

City were only occasionally showing signs of acclimatising to their harsh unwanted new surroundings. The fact was that there was no way they could play their way out of the Second Division.

Unless the Blues fought fire with fire, they would get nowhere fast so the autumnal purchase of former Huddersfield captain Andy Morrison – a snip at £80,000 – was looking like a wise move by Joe Royle. A natural warrior and beast of a defender, the fear he could instil in anyone not giving 100 per cent on a match day or in training was, itself, worth its weight in gold.

The arrival of long-time leaders Stoke City to Maine Road for the last game of the year on 28 December, therefore, gave the Blues the chance to show that the previous win at Wrexham, hard-earned and unpleasant on the eye as it had been, was not just another flash in the pan but the start of something more solid to build on.

Stoke had their own agenda having been relegated on their own turf by the Blues the previous May in a humiliating 5-2 defeat. As Royle would often reiterate, the size of City's following during this season of purgatory was quite overwhelming for all concerned. This could work in two ways, Royle maintained, either as a dead weight around the neck or as a galvanising force.

'There is a certain element who are becoming very vociferous and very negative,' wrote Royle in his pre-match programme notes for Stoke. Continuing with the same theme, he said, 'I can understand why two chairmen and a succession of managers have been hounded out of this place.'

Perhaps shocked by the harshness of Royle's words, the crowd's reaction was exemplary. For the first time since the opening day victory over Blackpool, there was evidence of just how the home crowd's influence on the legs and minds of the City players could work greatly to the team's benefit.

Stoke had deservedly led the division for most of the season but, entering this match in third place, they were waning under the pressure of a lengthy period out ahead of the pack.

With more than 30,000 inside Maine Road, it was the home side who had the better of the opening passage of play and, although City had a goal disallowed when Taylor's tenth-minute header was ruled out by a fussy linesman, Stoke gradually took command and took the lead with a well-worked goal after half an hour.

City's defence appeared to stand and watch as Sigurdsson rose to head in after a simple move had carved the Blues open down the right flank. Failure to build on Wrexham would surely end the Blues' hopes of promotion before Big Ben chimed in the New Year. Something had to change – and quickly.

Royle made a vital tactical move at half-time, bringing on Shaun Goater to accompany Paul Dickov and Gareth Taylor up front and taking off Ian Bishop. Once again City tore into the visitors and this time their energetic play reaped immediate dividends.

A mistake at the back produced a scuffle between Goater and the pressurised keeper Carl Muggleton, allowing the ball to be rolled across the area for Dickov to tap in. Maine Road erupted and, with the forceful and noisy backing of the crowd, City grew in stature and confidence.

Stoke were pinned back for long periods, but managed to hold on until five minutes from time, when Dickov's speculative cross from far out on the left was headed in majestically by Taylor – his first goal in City colours since a £400,000 transfer from Sheffield United eight weeks earlier.

With Maine Road in a tumult of noise, the visitors could not muster an answer to this late surge and City captured what was at the time a prize scalp.

The manager's concerns about the fans had been answered in no uncertain terms. The wall of noise created in the second half had persuaded the players to give everything.

'The crowd will remember the second half for the guts and passion we showed and football we played at times. In the end, justice was done,' said the City boss afterwards.

The win felt far grander than it perhaps deserved. This had been no ordinary league win, it had been a cup final with a victory uniting players and supporters to produce an irresistible tour de force.

As the crowd trickled out of the old stadium, a palpable sense of belief was in the air. Everyone had done their bit. The feeling was very much that this could be the catalyst to set the Blues on a run towards glorious promotion in May – all of which was proved correct, although the manner that it would finally be achieved could not have been imagined on that biting December evening.

v Borussia Monchengladbach

7 March 1979 and 19 March 1979
UEFA Cup fourth round. Attendance: 39,005

MANCHESTER CITY:	BORUSSIA MONCHENGLADBACH:
Corrigan	Kneib
Donachie	Schaffer
Power	Hannes
Reid	Schafer
Watson	Klinkhammer
Booth	Bruns
Channon	Simonsen
Viljoen	Kulik (Wohlers 75)
Kidd	Del'Haye
Hartford	Nielsen
Barnes	Lienen (Gores 80)

WHEN CITY pulled Borussia Monchengladbach out of the hat for the quarter-final of what was still a major European competition, there was a genuine feeling that if the Blues could see off the Bundesliga giants, the trophy was there for the taking.

It was, however, the worst draw possible with several lesser lights still in the competition plus fellow English side West Bromwich Albion.

'Kevin Keegan, the English jewel in the crown of West German football is backing Manchester City to topple Borussia Monchengladbach in the UEFA Cup quarter final' announced the *Daily Express* on Friday 19 January, the day of the draw for the last eight for what was then the third of UEFA's yearly tournaments.

There was no denying City's opponents were one of the strongest teams in (then West) Germany and one of European football's traditional powerhouses.

Having already dealt comfortably with Twente Enschede, Standard Liege and AC Milan, hopes were high that City could salvage some glory from a season that had flopped badly.

Malcolm Allison's so called 'Second Coming' had proved to be a disaster and the Blues, tipped at the start of the campaign to be in the final shake-up for the title, were well adrift in lower mid-table.

The Germans, who had seen off Sturm Graz, Benfica and Slask Wroclaw to reach the last eight, were not without their problems either, slowly decreasing in power from the mighty outfit which had dominated the Bundesliga and jousted with Liverpool in UEFA and European Cup finals in the early 1970s (many still remembered with awe Keegan's last match in a Liverpool shirt as he gave the limpet marking of German stopper Bertie Vogts the run-around in Rome as Liverpool took the European crown in 1977).

Typical of Allison's approach in this period, faced with the dilemma of who was to replace the suspended Gary Owen (Owen had kung-fu kicked his way into a red card in Liege in the second round in the previous November), the maverick Allison opted to give Nicky Reid a debut at the age of 18 and ask him to mark the then European Footballer of the Year and Denmark national hero Allan Simonsen who was in his final season with Monchengladbach.

This, with Colin Bell and Kaziu Deyna, European veterans both, ready to come in for Owen and shore up the middle of the park if need be but neither option appealed to City's maverick coach.

Allison was a gambler and Reid was chosen. If it worked, it would be the work of a genius – if it failed it had been a brave decision to place such faith in youth so who could argue?

Reid played well enough in the first leg, considering the almighty burden bestowed upon him (Allison would similarly launch 16-year-old youth team captain Tommy Caton at the start of the next season), but City struggled to get through a rugged, determined German rearguard, backed by some great keeping from the giant Wolfgang Kneib.

There was real optimism, however, when former record signing Mike Channon put the Blues ahead after 25 minutes as the ex-Southampton striker capitalised on a loose ball in the box to rasp the ball past Kneib.

Unable to build on the lead, City were pegged back midway through the second period, when Simonsen's trickery on the wing opened up a chance for Ewald Lienen to clip the ball past Joe Corrigan for a priceless away goal.

The Germans tested Corrigan towards the end and Bruns's shot smacked off a post with City losing their shape and probably realising the tie was now firmly tipped in favour of the West Germans.

Even the normally mild-mannered Paul Power started a multi-player punch-up after a robust challenge on the Monchengladbach keeper as tempers threatened to boil over completely.

Borussia were not entirely alone in being pleased with the 1-1 draw. Allison, though, later commented, 'I would not say they were defensive, let's just say they got all 11 players behind the ball every time we came within 40 yards of their goal!'

The second leg, played in front of a Bokelberg Stadium packed to its 35,000 capacity, saw a gutsy City performance undone by sheer bad luck just before the interval. With the game ebbing and flowing and little to choose between the sides, Tony Henry sent a screaming shot onto the Borussia post in the 44th minute.

Picking up the loose ball, the Germans swept straight upfield and Kulik buried a shot to send his side in at the interval one up.

Allison would later say that 'the goal just before half-time broke our neck' but in truth City were to take quite a hammering in the second half, with the Danes Simonsen and Kalle Del'Haye attacking down either flank in mesmerising fashion.

By the 72nd minute City were three down to goals from Bruns and the menacing Del'Haye and heading for the exit.

It had been a titanic struggle but the Germans on this form held just too many aces for the Blues to deal with. Deyna's belated introduction for the struggling Nicky Reid, however, sparked a revival and his sweetly struck volley from Channon's pass brought City back into the game, if not really the tie.

City had been steamrollered in the second half by the all-out attacking wing play of Udo Lattek's Borussia, who would go on to win the competition against Eintracht Frankfurt in the final.

It had been a fantastic journey through to the quarter-finals, illuminating what might have been in an increasingly disappointing season. No one present at either match against Borussia Monchengladbach could possibly have realised at the time how many years of torment were to follow before the Blues once again graced the playing fields of continental Europe.

v Birmingham City 3-1

25 August 1973
First Division
Attendance: 34,178

MANCHESTER CITY:	BIRMINGHAM CITY:
Corrigan	Latchford
Book (Carradous)	Martin
Donachie	Pendrey
Doyle	Page
Booth	Hynd
Oakes	Burns
Summerbee	Campbell
Bell	Francis
Lee	Latchford
Law	Hatton
Marsh	Taylor

AFTER A decade scoring goals for Manchester United under the nickname The King, it was hard to imagine Denis Law ever playing for City again. A lot of water had passed under the bridge and Law was an Old Trafford legend. Besides, surely, by 1974, he was over the hill?

City boss Johnny Hart thought differently and in what was either a stroke of genius or act of condemnation, when he was made aware of Law's availability, he moved swiftly for a player he had once called his team-mate back in 1960/61.

Law didn't need to be convinced. Controversial, yes, but it had been made clear he was surplus to requirements in United's ageing team by manager Tommy Docherty and with a minimum of upheaval physically (though a maximum change mentally), he swapped red for blue and came back to the club he'd played just one full season for.

'It will be really great going back to my old club. But I can tell you that if City hadn't made a bid for me, I would have packed in the game,' said Law on the eve of the 1973/74 season, his last in English football. He had signed for a single season, with an option for a second, after surprisingly being given a free from the Reds.

Hart admitted taking a gamble on the man he wanted to join Colin Bell, Francis Lee, Mike Summerbee and the unsettled Rodney Marsh to make

87

an irresistible front line, but he believed not only that it would work, but that the City fans would accept the Law man back.

'Both Denis and myself stand to be shot at,' added Hart, alluding to the throw of the dice he was taking.

Immediately Marsh was removed from the transfer list and Law scored his first goal for the first team in a pre-season game against Oldham. It was the best possible start and if there were to be any dissenters, they were quickly silenced as the old pro showed he still possessed the same predatory instincts he had always had. His pace was gentler, but his mind was still razor sharp.

City launched the season with a mundane 1-0 home defeat against Burnley in the Charity Shield, but, as the sun came out over an expectant Maine Road a week later, the scene was set for a memorable performance and a vintage display from Law.

More than 34,000 made their way to the ground to witness Law's second coming and if there were any doubts about his loyalties, they were ended after his first 90 minutes against Birmingham.

Those who had questioned the acquisition were soon singing his praises after great work from Marsh and Lee down the left flank opened up the visitors' defence. The cross into the box found Bell who headed the ball into Law's path and the Scot span acrobatically to volley home with his right foot to demonstrate he'd lost none of his predatory instincts.

The North Stand erupted and all connections with the Reds were forgotten as Law celebrated with his trademark one raised arm celebration.

By half-time Birmingham were level after Trevor Francis, later to do much the same for City in one injury-plagued season, ran at the hosts' rearguard down the right flank and, beating them with a combination of pace and trickery, crossed low for Bob Hatton to deflect into the net.

In the second half City quickly regained the initiative. First, from Summerbee's corner, the Birmingham defence failed to clear the ball and it fell to Bell on the edge of the box. The England midfielder controlled the cross on his chest, went past the lunge of a defender and despatched it calmly past Dave Latchford for 2-1.

Then came the moment of the match. With Birmingham beginning to tire in the sun and City beginning to showboat somewhat, the ball fell to Rodney Marsh on the Kippax side of Birmingham's penalty area.

The mercurial forward brought the ball under control and waited for the defender, Roger Hynd, to face him properly, before wafting his foot over the ball, as if he didn't quite know what he was going to do with it.

Suitably off balance, Hynd fell to one side as Marsh dummied again and went the other way, crossing to the far post with his left foot, where Law climbed to head home his second of the game to spark feverish celebrations around Maine Road.

'The perfect finish to Denis Law's perfect day,' chirruped a young John Motson on that night's *Match of the Day* and few could argue.

Law's double set City off to a great start to the season, which would ultimately end trophy-less, despite a heroic run to the League Cup Final, where Wolves' understudy keeper Gary Pearce would play a blinder to keep out Law, Marsh and the rest of the five-man City attack in a heartbreaking performance that resulted in a 2-1 win for the Black Country side.

Law's transfer to City was a wise move by Hart, who had been replaced by Ron Saunders who in turn was replaced by Tony Book. Dennis's 12 goals in 29 matches was proof that the gamble had been worthwhile and though his legs would eventually fail him, he would still write his name into the club's history books and send a dagger to the hearts of his former employers when he instinctively summoned the strength for one last flick off his boot to back-heel the ball into the net at Old Trafford one more time – but this time with a sky blue jersey on – effectively confirming United's relegation.

The goal would be his last act in league football before the season came to a fitting end playing in the dark blue of Scotland in the 1974 World Cup finals in West Germany, where the Scots remained unbeaten, but went out after games against Zaire, Brazil and Yugoslavia.

The King was dead – long live the King.

v Middlesbrough 4-0

21 January 1976
League Cup semi-final second leg
Attendance: 44,426

MANCHESTER CITY:	MIDDLESBROUGH:
Corrigan	Platt
Barrett	Craggs
Donachie	Cooper
Doyle	Souness
Clements	Boam
Oakes	Maddren
Power	Murdoch (McAndrew)
Keegan	Brine
Royle	Hickton
Hartford	Mills
Barnes	Armstrong

THERE WAS a time when City looked like making the League Cup their specialist competition. During the 1970s, the Blues made it to three finals in six years. City carried off the trophy twice, beating West Brom and Newcastle, though nobody knew the triumph in 1976 would be the last piece of silverware the club would win for an astonishing 35 years!

To get to the aforementioned final, City had struggled past an odd variety of sides, from Norwich and Nottingham Forest in the early rounds to the sound thrashing of Manchester United in the fourth – the game when Colin Bell suffered his horrific knee injury – and a 4-2 win over Fourth Division Mansfield Town in the quarter-finals.

This set up a semi-final over two legs with Jackie Charlton's Middlesbrough, a team hewn out of the same stubborn, no-nonsense granite as their bull-necked manager who had been the rock of Leeds United's defence during his distinguished playing career.

Boro won the first leg 1-0 in a tight and passionate game at Ayresome Park, setting up the Maine Road second leg beautifully. The stage was set for a memorable night and the Blues would not disappoint.

City boss Tony Book kept faith with the side that had beaten West Ham 3-0 the previous Saturday, which meant there was no recall for the fit-again defensive lynchpin Tommy Booth.

The much-needed confidence-booster over the Hammers ended a run of four successive 1-0 defeats and restored the players' faith at a point where things could have turned decidedly pear-shaped.

Boro had come out of the Second Division on the back of a stern defence that gave little away, so most pundits felt that City were up against it to make it to their third League Cup Final in six years. What followed on the night of the second leg was a City performance that had the old ground in raptures.

With injury and suspension robbing City of three England internationals, the Blues not only made up the deficit, they pulverised their north-eastern opponents with a four-goal salvo.

It was a trio of youngsters who took the plaudits on the night: Paul Power, who had played his first full game in the first leg, Ged Keegan, playing only his sixth full game for the seniors and Peter Barnes, at 19, about to embark on a glittering international career. Barnes, incidentally, had broken his nose against West Ham four days earlier, but it wouldn't affect him in the slightest for this match.

The tie swung City's way right from the start. The early breakthrough, so vital in such finely balanced ties, came as Barnes chased a seemingly over-hit cross by Asa Hartford with the visitors' defence anticipating it would go out of play.

However, the young winger sprinted in on the blind side and hit an instant left-foot cross on the run back into the box where Keegan headed thunderously past Jim Platt.

City nudged ahead on aggregate after only 11 minutes of a breathless start. Colin Barrett's cross appeared to touch Keegan's hand as it slid across the edge of the box, but the referee waved play-on and Alan Oakes hit a screaming left-foot drive into the Middlesbrough net.

The inexperience of Power almost let the Teessiders back into the game on 17 minutes when David Armstrong seized on a weak back pass, rounded Corrigan and slapped his shot onto the post. With the tie on a knife-edge, that coat of paint effectively sealed the fate of Big Jack's men.

This was to be City's night, and, as Craggs lost a square ball from Murdoch in no man's land, Barnes stormed through the middle to sweep the doubts away with the third of the evening, planting a low shot past the advancing Platt.

The final goal, a minute from time, was a neat replica of the third, as the hapless Craggs again was to blame when he sent a poor pass into the path of Joe Royle who strode forward to belt his shot past Platt and so continue his record of scoring in every round.

There were 11 heroes in blue shirts that night with all the youngsters impressive throughout, but Royle, Oakes, Asa Hartford, Kenny Clements and Joe Corrigan were all in the frame for man of the match honours. Big Joe left the pitch in tears. 'The emotion was just too much for me,' explained City's giant keeper.

Long-serving skipper Mike Doyle drove his side on relentlessly from the back in what many considered was his greatest game for the Blues – quite a compliment considering the amount of fantastic games he played in sky blue.

Tony Book, who had led City to all their earlier triumphs, was especially proud to be given the chance to repeat those efforts as manager and joked, 'Wait until we get our first team out!'

He added, 'If I had to pick out one man, I would nominate Gerard Keegan. When kids come into the team and play like that, it gives you a feeling you can't explain.'

Jack Charlton was not in the best of moods after the game and claimed that City had scored four goals with their only four shots of the evening, but then, Big Jack had the ability to turn a pint of milk sour with an unsavoury glance if he so wished.

Ged Keegan would hold onto his place for the final against Newcastle United and Barnes would once again reveal his rich promise with the opening goal on an afternoon still feted to this day by Blues supporters for Dennis Tueart's unforgettable overhead kick that sealed a 2-1 win over the Magpies – but that, of course, is an entirely different story.

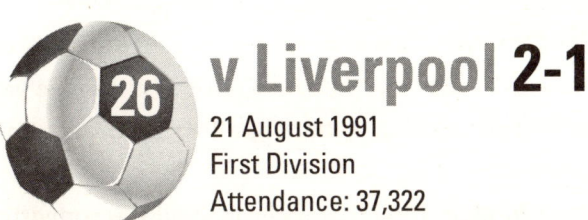

26 v Liverpool 2-1

21 August 1991
First Division
Attendance: 37,322

MANCHESTER CITY:	LIVERPOOL:
Coton	Grobbelaar
Hill	Ablett
Pointon	Burrows
Reid (Heath)	Nicol
Curle	Whelan
Redmond	Wright (Marsh)
White	Saunders
Brightwell	Houghton
Quinn	McManaman
Megson	Barnes (Walters)
Brennan	McMahon

CITY HAD begun the 1991/92 season with a 1-0 away win at Coventry, thanks to Niall Quinn's headed goal, and went into the first home game of the season against Liverpool determined to end a nightmarish run against the Merseysiders on home soil.

With nine defeats in the last ten home games against the Reds – and 33 goals conceded during that time – City fans turned up expecting the usual Maine Road thrashing. It wasn't a defeatist attitude, just an acceptance that Liverpool had been a class apart from the Blues for more than a decade and, for whatever reason, they clearly relished playing on Maine Road's wide open spaces with City being the proud owners of the biggest pitch in England at that time.

But with City now player-managed by ex-Evertonian Peter Reid, this would be a game where the Blues would at least give a decent account of themselves.

Too many 4-0 scorelines had gone in favour of the visitors in this fixture and Reid was determined that the experienced and workmanlike side he'd fashioned over the summer wouldn't lie down and roll over for anyone – least of all the fierce rivals of his former employers – something that also applied to Gary Megson, Neil Pointon and Adrian Heath who were also in the starting XI that day.

A feature of Reid's City team was that they were seldom found wanting when they had a battle on their hands – the manager managed to get the best out of his squad and the fact that he was lining up alongside them in matches must have helped.

It was a dry, bright early August evening and a crowd in excess of 37,000 took the opportunity to welcome the Blues back home after the summer break.

While the visitors had added the likes of Mark Wright and Dean Saunders to an already impressive squad, Reid's main summer signing had been Keith Curle from Wimbledon for £2.5m – a price tag that made the former Dons skipper the most expensive defender in English football at that time.

He would play his part, too, in a great all-round performance from the Blues who had a touch of steel about them for the first time in many years. They needed it with Liverpool packed full of stellar names and exciting attacking talent.

City tore into Liverpool from the first minute, never allowing players who could hurt you if you allowed them too much time and space and as a result, the dangerous John Barnes and an emerging Steve McManaman weren't allowed time to settle into their stride.

With Wright struggling to contain the flailing limbs of Niall Quinn and Ian Brightwell's midfield energy snuffing out the usually dominant Steve McMahon, City had set the foundations to go on and beat Liverpool at home for the first time since Boxing Day 1985.

A constant aerial threat, it was Quinn who provided the opening from which City finally made the breakthrough. In the 30th minute he lobbed a glorious pass over the top of David Burrows into the path of David White whose pace had already taken him clear of the rest of the Liverpool defence.

A slide-rule finish past Reds keeper Bruce Grobbelaar put the Blues one up and sent Maine Road wild.

Liverpool huffed and puffed but Tony Coton was rarely threatened and midway through the second half, the same devastating combination of Quinn and White helped City double their advantage though not without more than a touch of controversy.

Quinn's flick-on sent White hurtling towards the Liverpool box with Wright once again trailing in his wake. As the City striker looked up, he unleashed an unstoppable drive, which rocketed past Grobbelaar and hit the underside of the bar before bouncing away to safety.

Had it crossed the line? There was a moment's confusion and it seemed to take an age for referee Paul Vanes to make his mind up, but after checking with his linesman, the goal was given and the packed Kippax went crazy as the official pointed to the centre spot. White was duly mobbed by his team-mates and the Blues were on the brink of a famous win.

It wasn't over. City were 2-0 up, but there was still time for the almost inevitable Liverpool comeback, inspired by the impressive McManaman who had at last broken free of his shackles. The young winger pulled a goal back with a diving header not long after and then, as City seemed to be home and dry, Andy Hill's outstretched leg brought down £2.9m signing Dean Saunders – a boyhood City fan.

Penalty to the Reds and agony for the home fans who knew the win had seemingly been in the bag. The Welshman dusted himself down and was perhaps mindful of Niall Quinn's penalty save against him the previous season when Derby were relegated – yes, that was striker Quinn in goal covering for the dismissed Tony Coton.

Whatever was going through his mind, he walloped his penalty against the underside of the bar – but there was to be no repeat decision from the referee as the ball bounced clear without going over the line, proving perhaps that lightning really doesn't strike the same place twice.

Maine Road erupted and the Blues ran the remaining minutes down to claim a 2-1 win. The hex had finally been laid to rest and a 3-2 win over Crystal Palace the following Saturday would put the Blues top of the table with a 100 per cent record. David White, meanwhile, would hit another double against Liverpool in the return match at Anfield, confirming an end to the era where Liverpool only had to show up to guarantee victory over the Blues.

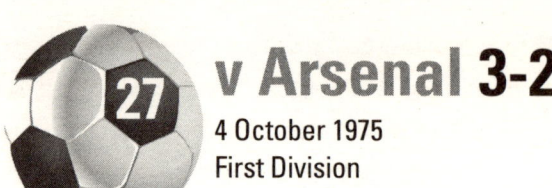

v Arsenal 3-2

4 October 1975
First Division
Attendance: 24,928

MANCHESTER CITY:	ARSENAL:
Corrigan	Rimmer
Clements	Rice
Donachie	Nelson
Doyle	Kelly (Rostron)
Watson	Simpson
Oakes	O'Leary
Hartford	Ball
Bell	Cropley
Royle	Stapleton
Marsh	Kidd
Tueart (Power)	Brady

WITH A solid first season under his belt, manager Tony Book continued to hone his team with one or tweaks here and there. Mike Summerbee had moved on while Kenny Clements had been fast-tracked into the first team after impressing at reserve level. Joe Corrigan had been restored as the first-choice goalkeeper after slimming down and getting his act together and there was a feeling that this City team may be able to bring some silverware home that season.

In contrast, Arsenal's fortunes had withered after their great double-winning era and the team was slowing down considerably by the mid-1970s. Youthful replacements such as Liam Brady, Frank Stapleton and David O'Leary were taking time to bed in and old campaigners like Ball, Simpson, Kelly and Pat Rice were beginning to wind down their illustrious careers.

It was at this crossroads that a City side with a complete inability to win away from home arrived in north London one sunny autumnal afternoon. City had already lost 2-0 at Coventry, 1-0 at West Ham, 1-0 at Derby and by the same score at Aston Villa by the time the Gunners fixture arrived – though by contrast were carrying a burgeoning reputation as the division's best home side.

But by losing all of their away games and without scoring a single goal, Book knew he would never be able to fashion a title challenging side

Niall Quinn – twice on the mark against Sunderland in 1991

May 1985 – more than 20,000 City fans celebrate on the Maine Road pitch after promotion is secured against Charlton Athletic

Mike Channon in 1978 – on target in the 6-2 romp over Chelsea at Maine Road

1969 FA Cup success: Alan Oakes, Neil Young, Glyn Pardoe and keeper Harry Down celebrate the 1-0 win over Leicester City

1956 FA Cup Final: Concern for Bert Trautmann who has broken his neck after a clash with Birmingham's Peter Murphy

Ian Bishop – an integral part of City's 5-1 win over United in 1989

More than 10,000 City fans travelled to Stoke to see the debut of Trevor Francis in 1981 – he didn't disappoint, scoring twice

1976 League Cup Final v Newcastle. Dennis Tueart pats goalscorer Peter Barnes on the back as City beat Newcastle United 2-1 to lift the 1976 League Cup

Joe Mercer congratulates Mike Summerbee after the 1969 FA Cup Final win over Leicester City

Francis Lee in action against West Ham in 1972 – oddly, he wasn't among the scorers in a 4-3 win

City captain Roy Paul shows off the FA Cup in 1956 after the 3-1 victory over Birmingham City with team-mates (l-r) Bobby Johnstone, Dave Ewing, Don Revie, Ken Barnes, Roy Clarke and Jack Dyson

1981 FA Cup semi-final: Paul Power battles with Ipswich Town's John Wark

1970: Tony Book collects the European Cup Winners' Cup after a 2-1 win over Gornik – and no, that's not Steve McClaren with the brolly!

1979: Borussia Monchengladbach under pressure as Peter Barnes and Brian Kidd scramble for possession

until he cured his team's travel sickness. It was partly a hangover from the previous campaign and perhaps partly a mental block.

To add to the problems, the Blues had failed to score on their past three visits to Arsenal's fortress.

The Blues' previous midweek fixture had seen a definite upturn in fortunes, however. This had happened most unexpectedly at Stamford Bridge, but in a game against Norwich City during a second replay in the League Cup. A stunning 6-1 mauling of the Canaries, which included a fine hat-trick from Dennis Tueart, gave the Blues the confidence they needed going to a ground where they habitually lost.

Despite the six scored against the Canaries, Book's men had to prove they could hurt teams in the league, too. In mid-table, City arrived four places higher than Arsenal for this game that saw the Gunners in 15th.

The hosts had only won two of their opening nine games, but they had also lost only two and conceded few goals. So, taking everything into account, City surprised even their own travelling supporters at Highbury by racing into a three-goal lead before the second half was two minutes old. It was typical City! From one extreme to the other, the Blues had now bagged nine goals in slightly over a game and a half in two London matches. The floodgates had well and truly opened.

With thoughts of win bonuses and adulatory press reports beginning to occupy the players' minds, things then took a change for the worse as the hosts began to claw their way back into the game. By the end, the Blues were doggedly hanging on for a 3-2 victory but it was one they would successfully see out.

This absorbing game centred on two titanic struggles in the middle of the park, which would eventually settle the match in City's favour.

The first was between Ball and Doyle. Doyle enthused afterwards in typical fashion, 'It was nothing!' while Ball, still limping an hour after the game had ended, said, 'I heard a thump, felt a thud and thought that my leg was broken!'

The second, between the young Brady and the wily Hartford, raged all afternoon, culminating in a booking for the City midfielder. By then Hartford had already got his name on the scoresheet and Brady's role had become somewhat peripheral to proceedings.

City sparked into action first, Rodney Marsh and Willie Donachie linking well down the left flank. Bell's far-post flick was headed goalwards by Hartford, who saw his first effort saved by the stretching Arsenal keeper Jimmy Rimmer. The City man made no mistake with his second bite, tucking the ball away under the crossbar.

City took the game beyond the Gunners with two rapid-fire goals either side of half-time, the first something of a collector's item, a 25-yard rocket by Joe Royle which fairly flew past Rimmer and the second an ungainly side header by Marsh – hardly renowned for his aerial ability – from Bell's accurate pass.

With City still busy congratulating themselves on this decisive change of fortune, Ball pulled one back from 20 yards out (his leg still working at this point) to give his shell-shocked team a glimmer of hope.

Arsenal then played out the rest of the game by laying siege to the City goal. But while Brady's effort was disallowed, the industrious Ball sent Alex Cropley though to jink past the diving Corrigan and tuck the ball home to rouse the disappointing 24,928 Highbury crowd.

With Paul Power on for the injured Tueart, City just about managed to steady the ship and held out for the win.

The effect on the Blues' away fortunes was also interesting, as a string of score draws replaced the earlier defeats and an emphatic 4-0 win at Wolves, involving a comedy goal as players and referee fell over each other as the ball swung into the box – you really had to see it to believe it – underlined the point that City's away hoodoo had been well and truly put to bed at Highbury.

Or so we all thought … fast forward 38 years before the Blues next enjoyed a win away to Arsenal!

v Chelsea 4-1

28

16 September 1978
First Division
Attendance: 29,980

MANCHESTER CITY:	CHELSEA:
Corrigan	Bonetti
Donachie	Locke
Power	Harris
Viljoen	Lewington
Watson	Hay
P. Futcher	Wicks
Channon	Swain
Owen	R Wilkins (Britton)
R. Futcher	Langley
Hartford	Stanley
Barnes	McKenzie

THIS WAS a pivotal campaign for Tony Book's City who were reaching a crossroads under his stewardship. It was either time to kick on or ship out because the Blues had become something of a nearly team – nearly winning the league twice in the past two years but still light years behind the seemingly indestructible machine that was Liverpool FC.

City went into the 1978/79 season attempting to keep up an increasingly high standard. The previous five seasons had seen finishes of 14th, eighth, eighth, second and fourth.

The Blues were now established as regular league title challengers with a big, expensively assembled squad and expectations to match.

Despite an August Maine Road drubbing from Liverpool (this, as previously illustrated, was a regular occurrence whatever City's form), the Blues found themselves reasonably placed in tenth after the first five games had been played. They approached a tricky trip to Stamford Bridge on the back of an encouraging midweek draw in Enschede in the UEFA Cup.

Chelsea, still looking for a home goal and a home point, looked ripe for the picking. The Pensioners were marooned in the bottom three and already looking like a side in for a long, hard season and so it would prove.

City had drawn both away games at Derby and Norwich 1-1 so the scene was set and, for Ron Futcher in particular, it was to be perhaps the greatest day of his career in what would prove a short and otherwise uneventful City stint.

Seen as the makeweight in the £350,000 transfer that took his brother Paul from Luton Town to Maine Road, Ron was viewed primarily as the insurance policy, brought along to keep his brother from being homesick, while Paul was the England centre-half in waiting and tipped by some to be a future Three Lions skipper.

It had been the same story when they set off for Luton from Chester together and now brother Paul commanded more than two-thirds of the huge transfer fee that had brought them back north.

Thanks to an injury to Brian Kidd, however, both brothers would play in this game and it would be Ron who would emerge the star turn.

City, who had thrashed Chelsea 6-2 at Maine Road a year earlier, came out wearing the 1970s classic white away kit with the black and red diagonal sash, itself in those days a hark back to the early part of the decade when City set the sartorial pace with a succession of similarly avant-garde kits.

As the teams ran out at Stamford Bridge into bright sunshine, both sets of fans were hopeful that their team might finally click into gear but it didn't take long for the visitors to suggest it was they, rather than their hosts, who might actually show their true mettle.

With the creative midfield trio of Gary Owen, Asa Hartford and Colin Viljoen taking the game by the scruff of the neck right from the start, the crowd did not have long to wait for the first goal.

With the home fans still laughing at Peter Barnes' attempt to control a high pass on the halfway line, former Ipswich Town favourite Viljoen lifted a clever ball over the statuesque home defence for Channon to race through clear on goal. He kept his head and then drilled a low shot past Peter Bonetti to put City ahead.

The Blues were knocking the ball around with practice match composure and a terrific move started with Channon bursting down the right before finding Ron Futcher who in turn fed Hartford whose 25-yard daisy cutter rattled a post with Chelsea well and truly on the rack.

But the Pensioners rallied with Lee going close with a diving header and then Ron 'Chopper' Harris firing a long-range shot that whistled past the post not long after.

Had one of those gone in instead of wide, Chelsea would surely have gone on to win this contest – but City struck again before the break to give themselves breathing space.

Joe Corrigan's prodigious punt downfield was carried on by the gusting wind, found Channon who glanced the ball into the patch of Ron Futcher, who sliced through the remnants of the defence and tucked away a fierce right-foot shot for his first City goal.

With Chelsea's demoralised players looking to the tunnel for half-time resuscitation, Futcher pounced again after 44 minutes after more fine work by Channon and Hartford set up the striker to bury a low shot past Bonetti with the calmness of a natural born finisher. Now three goals to the good, there was no way City would pass up this opportunity to travel back north with maximum points.

It was not long into the second half before City had worked a fourth. Barnes whipped in a corner, which was not properly cleared. Hartford picked up the loose ball and angled it back into the box, where Ron Futcher stooped bravely to head his hat-trick goal home. This was not just any old treble, either, but the textbook classic of right foot, left foot and a header.

City seemed to declare at four, letting the home side into the game more, and Corrigan was forced to earn his corn with a number of saves, before a header from Gary Stanley crept past him after hitting the post. Chelsea left the field heads bowed, as Ron Futcher left the pitch, for once, as the name on everyone's lips.

He would finish the season with seven goals from ten starts – a fair return by anyone's standards – before heading off six months later to a new career in America with Minnesota Kicks.

It is doubtful anything ever topped this match in a career that sadly faded into obscurity as the years went on.

v Tottenham Hotspur 5-2

22 October 1994
Premier League
Attendance: 25,473

MANCHESTER CITY:	TOTTENHAM HOTSPUR:
Dibble	Walker
Edghill	Kerslake
Curle	Edinburgh
Brightwell	Popescu
Phelan	Scott
Flitcroft	Campbell
Lomas	Dozzell (Hazard)
Summerbee	Barmby
Beagrie	Klinsmann
Quinn	Sheringham
Walsh	Dumitrescu

A S THE players trooped off the Maine Road pitch at the end of this rain-lashed game, John Motson declared to the watching *Match of the Day* millions that this had been one of the best he could remember covering for the BBC.

'This was a throwback to how the game used to be played,' he chirruped as Maine Road stood and clapped to a man. For those lucky enough to be in the ground that day – the old ground's capacity had been severely reduced owing to the rebuilding of the Kippax – it would be a game that would live long in the memory. And Motson, veteran of countless televised matches, was right.

This was an intriguing game. Two teams in mid-table with aspirations of better things and both having strengths – City were playing some mouth-watering stuff at Maine Road where the Blues had won three and drawn twice so far, scoring an average close to three per game. The visitors had already picked up ten points from a possible 15 on the road so, as the old saying goes, something had to give.

Spurs, under the tutelage of their former midfielder Osvaldo Ardiles, were as committed to attacking football as City were under Brian Horton and the match proved to be a monument to the respective managers' principles.

In unrelenting rain, the ebb and flow of the first half produced four goals and a welter of untaken chances as both teams slugged it out, blow for blow.

City struck first as a right-wing cross was half cut out by a young Sol Campbell after 16 minutes, but, as the defender lost his bearings, ex-Tottenham favourite Paul Walsh nipped in and tucked the ball away low to keeper Ian Walker's left.

Spurs hit back quickly. With their midfield busy weaving intricate patterns, looking for an opening, one of the more incisive of these allowed Jurgen Klinsmann to slip past the City defence, where he was unceremoniously upended by Andy Dibble, who had been sent off the week before for a similar kamikaze challenge on Les Ferdinand at QPR.

Dibble survived with a yellow card and Romanian international Ilie Dumitrescu slotted the penalty away easily for the equaliser. Klinsmann celebrated as though he had scored while City's own German striker Uwe Rosler sat injured in the stands – you could imagine the possible headlines had he played!

Before the break, City had seemingly tied the game up and went in 3-1 up thanks to the wing play of Nicky Summerbee and, in particular, Peter Beagrie.

First Summerbee's perfectly flighted right-wing cross was headed goalwards by Paul Walsh, only for Walker to parry his effort out to Niall Quinn. The big Irishman nodded home from a prone position, risking injury from Scott's flailing boot for his sixth goal in six games.

Then Beagrie skipped past two defenders on the left, motored over the halfway line and passed inside to Quinn, who moved the ball on in one movement to the incoming Walsh. The momentum of his shot carried the ball into the net after Walker's half-save.

With the crowd – and John Motson – buzzing, the half-time whistle came as a rude intrusion on a superb spell of open football. But it was far from finished.

The two sides resumed this pleasing spectacle immediately after the break and with just 60 seconds of the second period played, Dumitrescu rolled in a second Spurs goal from Klinsmann's clever back-heel and the game was on a knife-edge once again.

It was the worst possible start for the Blues but the hosts soon regained the momentum. City charged back and, with Walsh weaving in and out on the left and Beagrie tormenting the Tottenham rearguard, they managed to plunder two more goals.

Beagrie, at his irrepressible best, left David Kerslake tackling fresh air before whipping in a cross that was headed home powerfully by Steve Lomas and then Walsh, enjoying his best game in City colours, set up Garry Flitcroft for the fifth.

He ran at the heart of the Spurs rearguard, drawing three defenders in the process before laying the ball off to Flitcroft who finished with a clinical drive past Walker.

More chances came and went but by this time the crowd were simply lapping up the one-touch football and basking in a performance that would warm the wet souls in their Kippax waterproofs on the way home.

City toyed with Spurs in the time that remained and the visitors, ultimately, concentrated more on damage limitation than imagining there was some way back in to this match and were probably happy to escape with a 5-2 defeat.

Although Brian Horton's side would never quite reach these heights again, a swashbuckling 4-3 win at QPR in the League Cup followed the Spurs win and Ardiles lost his job shortly after the Maine Road drubbing.

Walsh would later claim he had been spurred on by revenge over his former employers and his boss Horton reckoned football had been the winner on this occasion.

'The real winners were the paying public and the viewers around the world who watched the match on television,' said the City boss.

'You won't see a better game of soccer than that. There were great individual performances from players on both sides. It wasn't all about Paul Walsh because there were tremendous performances from players like Peter Beagrie and Stevie Lomas.

'But you cannot take it away from Walsh. Even as a kid he had a great heart but I don't think he has ever played better in his career than he has since the day he arrived at Maine Road.

'All credit to Spurs. They didn't try to shut up shop and stop us playing. They kept going forward looking for goals just like us.'

30 v Gornik Zabrze 2-1

European Cup Winners' Cup Final
29 April 1970. Praterstadion, Vienna, Austria
Attendance: 7,968

MANCHESTER CITY:	GORNIK ZABRZE:
Corrigan	Kostka
Book	Oslizlo
Pardoe	Florenski (Deyna)
Doyle (Bowyer)	Gorgon
Booth	Olek
Oakes	Latocha
Heslop	Szoltysik
Bell	Wilczek (Skowronek)
Lee	Szaryniski
Young	Banas
Towers	Lubanski

THE BLUES' triumph in Vienna remains the only European trophy the club have so far collected, but then again, only a handful can actually lay claim to a major European trophy.

In today's mad world of European football, where groups play out phases, losers go into another competition and the dear old Cup Winners' Cup no longer exists, City's success was won the old fashioned way, via random draws out of a hat and good old two-legged knockout rounds.

City qualified by winning the 1969 FA Cup and were playing in Europe for the second successive year after taking part in the European Cup the previous season, falling at the first hurdle.

That time, Malcolm Allison had boasted how his side would 'terrify Europe' only to see Turkish side Fenerbahce edge the tie 2-1 on aggregate in what was a major shock. The disappointment and embarrassment felt by the players was obvious and they were determined to prove that they were among the very best on the continent next time around.

The tournament began in earnest with a qualifying round between Rapid Vienna and Torpedo Moscow. Both games finished as draws with Vienna progressing to the next phase on the away goals rule.

The first round proper was then drawn and City couldn't have asked for a much tougher test, pitted away to Athletic Bilbao. Gornik

Zabrze of Poland drew Olympiakos of Greece and Rapid Vienna, with the added incentive of the final being in their home city, took on PSV Eindhoven.

City seemed to be on their way out when Bilbao opened up a 2-0 lead in the first leg, in Spain. The Blues pulled a goal back, but again went two goals behind with time rapidly running out but they didn't give up and a late strike from Tommy Booth and an own goal gave them a fantastic 3-3 draw. It was just the fillip they needed after Fenerbahce.

Gornik drew 2-2 in Greece while Rapid's hopes nosedived with a 2-1 home loss to PSV. Elsewhere, Belgians SK Lierse trounced Cypriots APOEL Nicosia 10-1, while Cardiff City thrashed Mjøndalen IF 7-1 in Norway and Rangers beat Steaua Bucharest 2-0 at Ibrox.

For the return at Maine Road, goals from Colin Bell, Alan Oakes and Ian Bowyer eased City into the second round 3-0 and 6-3 on aggregate. Gornik won 5-0 against Olympiakos; Cardiff completed the rout of the Norwegian minnows 5-1 at Ninian Park; Rangers held out for a 0-0 draw in Romania and Rapid dipped out 4-2 at PSV. The next round would prove equally fascinating.

The Blues were then pitted against the first round's top scorers, with the first leg away against Belgians SK Lierse, who had banged in 11 goals and were something of an unknown quantity.

A 19,000 crowd packed into the Herman Vanderpoortenstadion with the local hopes high of an upset. Franny Lee and Bell had other ideas, however, and City coasted home 3-0. Gornik saw off Glasgow Rangers 3-1 in Poland, while Göztepe of Turkey all but ended Cardiff's hopes with a 3-0 win.

The second legs would see the end of all British interest bar City, who finished off the job against Lierse by scoring five without reply in front of 26,486 fans at Maine Road. Cardiff made a valiant bid to overturn their deficit but 1-0 was not enough, while Rangers went down to the inspired Gornik 3-1.

Elsewhere, German outfit Schalke 04 and Portuguese side Academica edged through by winning their home legs, while AS Roma and PSV both won their legs 1-0 and Roma progressed on the toss of a coin. And people complain about penalty shoot-outs!

With just eight teams left, City were keen to avoid the big guns of Gornik, Schalke, Levski-Sofia and Roma, while hoping not to have to travel to Turkey again, this time to face Göztepe.

The draw was kind and the first leg of the quarter-final was in Portugal against the relatively unknown university side Academica Coimbra. Domestically, the Blues had also reached the League Cup Final and would play West Brom at Wembley just three days after the clash in Portugal. In the league, City were floundering in mid-table so the cup competitions took on extra importance.

The first leg was a tough, bruising encounter with plenty of gamesmanship and physical threat from Academica, but in front of 15,000 fans, City held their nerve to take a priceless 0-0 draw back to Maine Road.

Schalke produced the performance of the night, winning 3-1 in Zagreb, while Gornik lost 3-2 in Sofia and Roma beat Göztepe 2-0 in Italy.

Joe Mercer's side flew back into thick fog in the UK and had to land at Birmingham before being bussed to London. The whole country was in the grip of snow and ice and the League Cup Final was in some doubt, especially after the Horse of the Year Show had made mincemeat of the pitch days earlier.

It went ahead and City earned their first trophy of the season, beating the Baggies 2-1 in extra time with a goal from that renowned goal poacher Glyn Pardoe.

The Blues were to be pushed to the limit, however, in the return leg against Academica, with the end of normal time still not producing a goal. It had been a dogged display by the Portuguese but Tony Towers proved to be the hero on the night with a 119th-minute winner to send the Blues into the last four.

Gornik overturned their 3-2 loss to Sofia by winning 2-1 and progressing on away goals. Both Schalke and Roma won their ties with two-goal cushions to make up the final four.

Whoever City drew, it was going to be tough, but avoiding Roma and Gornik was paramount and the tie against Schalke, who had lost in a game to Shamrock Rovers in the first round, represented a decent chance of making the final.

City withstood fierce pressure in Germany, losing by a single goal while Roma and Gornik drew 1-1 in Rome. City turned on the style in the home leg in front of a full house at Maine Road and goals from Neil Young (two), Bell, Lee and Mike Doyle saw them home 5-1, with Schalke becoming the first side in five European ties to score in Moss Side.

With the away goal rule not counting in the last four, Roma led 1-0 in Poland and were set for a final showdown with City until legendary striker Wlodzimierz Lubanski scored a 90th-minute leveller to send the 100,000 crowd into raptures. He scored again three minutes into extra time but the Italians fought back to earn a 2-2 draw and a play-off in Strasbourg.

Another 1-1 draw meant the tie had to be settled by the toss of a coin. This time, Roma's luck ran out and Gornik progressed to the final, leaving the Italians heartbroken at their ludicrous exit.

The final, at the Praterstadion in Austria, was played in front of a paltry 7,968 fans, with the Poles unable to sell many tickets because of visa problems for their supporters and around 7,000 City fans travelling to Vienna to make up the majority of the crowd.

At this point, Corrigan believed that City's name was on the cup. 'The win over Schalke really set us up for Gornik,' he admitted. 'We had a great team, who had won the League Cup just three months earlier and we didn't fear anyone. It was our third major final in less than a year and everyone was up for the occasion.

'When we got to the stadium, we never really had any doubts that we wouldn't win.'

Controversially, the FA Cup Final replay between Leeds and Chelsea was held on the same night as the City v Gornik final, which meant that the game, which should have been a source of national pride, lost some of its prestige. Not to the City players or supporters, though.

There were just 7,968 fans inside the enormous Praterstadion, but what they lacked numerically, the Blues fans more than made up for vocally. 'They were fantastic,' Corrigan recalled fondly, 'and made it just like a home match for us.'

City were without Mike Summerbee for the game after he sustained a hairline fracture in the League Cup Final just a few months earlier while Gornik had won their place in the final courtesy of a coin toss having drawn both semi-final legs and a subsequent replay against Italian side AS Roma.

Prior to the game, the heavens over Vienna opened and the irony wasn't lost on Joe Corrigan. Nor, for that matter, was it lost on the rest of the Manchester City squad that were waiting patiently in the tunnel.

As each drop of rain fell before kick-off, it appeared as though the weather was going to scupper the chances of Joe Mercer's side.

After training on the Austrian pitch a day before the game, coach Malcolm Allison had given the head groundsman a back-hander to water the pitch so that the surface would accommodate City's slick passing and movement. The blue skies, however, would not last – far from it.

A deluge of rain started as City left the dressing room and didn't halt until the final whistle – the Manchester weather had followed the team across Europe – Allison's efforts had been in vain.

'We had all complained that the grass was too long,' recalled Corrigan, who during the 1969/1970 season had established himself as City's number one keeper.

'Malcolm decided to get around this by giving the groundsman a little something and later, when it started to rain we just laughed. It was the way Malcolm was.'

Mercer's side rewarded the City fans who had made the long journey to Austria with an outstanding first half display which saw them race in to a 2-0 interval lead.

Neil Young netted the opening goal from inside the six-yard area after Franny Lee had skipped past a challenge and forced a save from Hubert Kostka but Young was first to the loose ball and he tucked a shot past the keeper and into the net with only 12 minutes on the clock – it had been the perfect start. Then, moments before half-time, the same two players combined to double the Blues' lead at a crucial stage of the game.

Young picked up a loose ball midway in the Gornik half and splashed his way through the defence only to have his charge towards goal unceremoniously halted by the onrushing Kostka who mistimed his dive at Young's feet, resulting in a penalty.

Lee drilled the spot kick down the middle and Kostka made some contact with the ball but the power on the shot ensured it crossed the line to double the lead and give the Blues what proved to be an unassailable advantage.

As expected, a few tense moments followed in the second period and Gornik pulled a goal back in the 68th minute through Oslizlo but City had too much strength and Ian Bowyer, on for the injured Doyle, almost sneaked a third goal late in the game.

Ironically, when the final whistle blew, the rain stopped, too – wild celebrations followed. City also became only the second English club to have won a domestic trophy and European competition in the same season (Leeds were the first in 1968).

'The only thing I remember about their goal was that it came from a free kick and took a deflection into the path of the player who scored. There was nothing I could do about it,' said Corrigan.

Corrigan made just under 600 appearances for the Blues and won nine England caps. He finds it hard to name one abiding memory of that miserable night in Vienna, which was illuminated by the result.

But of that double cup-winning season, he finds it less difficult to pinpoint a recollection.

'It was just brilliant to play in such a good team,' Corrigan said. 'It was a fantastic year, both for myself and the club. I had just broken into City's team and also got into the England Under-23 side.'

'There was an air of confidence about the team and it was just a pleasure to be involved.'

City would reach the semi-final of the same competition the following season, losing out to Chelsea and the 'jinx' of no team ever successfully defending their title would continue until the Cup Winners' Cup was scrapped in 1999 – this despite the defending champions reaching the final eight times.

City finished tenth in the First Division in 1970 and will forever hold the record of the team finishing lowest in their domestic league after winning the Cup Winners' Cup, but when another trophy was paraded in Albert Square in front of thousands of ecstatic Blues, nobody cared about that, or any other statistic.

v Watford **3-0**

11 August 2001
First Division
Attendance: 33,939

MANCHESTER CITY:	WATFORD:
Nash	Baardsen
Charvet	Blondeau
Howey	Robinson
Pearce	Vega
Dunne	Galli
Wiekens	Nielsen
Granville	Hyde
Tiatto	Vernazza
Berkovic	Hughes
Goater	Gayle
Wanchope	Smith

HIS MOTHER warned him not to go near the main road, so Kevin Keegan informed the nation's media at his unveiling press conference, but for the first couple of years of his reign as Manchester City manager, the Blues' supporters were overjoyed he had as the former Liverpool, Hamburg and Newcastle legend transformed City from an ailing yo-yo club into one of the most attacking and attractive sides in any of England's four divisions. Keegan was damaged goods in many ways, seemingly all too quick to walk when the going got tough and emotional to the point that it was actually a weakness.

Who could forget his rant at Alex Ferguson as his Newcastle side tossed away a huge lead in the race for the title a few years earlier? He had lost the mind games and would be forever tarnished by his very public cracking under immense pressure. But that was then, this was now and the prospect of high octane football, plenty of goals and flair by the bucket-load meant Keegan was welcomed with open arms by City fans and a certain amount of disbelief that the Blues had really hooked a massive name to reignite the passion among the masses.

Keegan's first competitive game as City boss was always going to be an electrically-charged affair, and so it proved in a cracking game that few who attended will ever forget.

It was the start of a new, exciting era, with John Wardle and David Makin's financial backing and one of the country's most charismatic men at the helm. Heady days awaited the success-starved supporters at Maine Road who had backed the team in their thousands during 20 long barren years.

Only two of Keegan's new boys started, but both Stuart Pearce and Eyal Berkovic would have a major influence on a game that crackled with expectancy from start to finish.

The unusual Saturday evening kick-off seemed to play its part, too, with ITV Digital choosing to have the match start at 5pm, just as the other First Division fixtures finished, though with 4-0 victories for both Millwall and Bradford, plus a 5-0 win for Gillingham already recorded, it was unlikely the Blues would finish the day as the league leaders.

No matter. There was a carnival atmosphere, no doubt fuelled in some part by a long afternoon in the pub for some, but just plain old excitement for others. The nation was watching – were the unpredictable City and heart-on-sleeve Keegan a match made in heaven or a Nevada divorce waiting to happen?

With Maine Road rocking in the dusk and the floodlights gleaming on to a perfect pitch, City and Watford walked out to a deafening roar and Keegan took his place on the bench, waving to all four sides of the ground as the people of Manchester welcomed the man charged with waking a slumbering giant.

With Keegan choosing a 5-3-2 formation, Carlo Nash got the nod in goal with Laurent Charvet and Pearce the full-backs. A trio of experienced centre-halves – Richard Dunne, Steve Howey and Gerard Wiekens – completed the defence. Danny Tiatto, Danny Granville – both full-backs in their own right – flanked Berkovic in midfield and Paulo Wanchope and Shaun Goater were the strikers.

Watford, just as at the time of writing, had employed a former Chelsea idol as their manager but while Gianfranco Zola had the role in 2013, back then it was Gianluca Vialli in control.

The Hornets had arrived to spoil the party, but it quickly became clear that it was going to take a mammoth effort to repel the wave of optimism sweeping around Maine Road, backed up by a fluidity not seen for a number of years as the Blues launched a series of inventive attacks, almost exclusively prompted by the impressive Israeli Berkovic.

Somehow, Watford survived until the break with the score still 0-0. Their plan, whatever it was, was working and if they could survive an hour without conceding, they had a real chance of heading south with more than just a point as frustration would surely set in.

In fact, they were just two minutes away from the hour-mark when Charvet picked up Berkovic's clever ball on the right then sent over a delicious cross for Goater to crash home a header and send Maine Road wild. Relief all round.

The Blues had their tails up now and tore mercilessly at Watford's beleaguered rearguard and five minutes later Wanchope thumped a header against the bar then Berkovic collected the rebound, cleverly moving the ball around defender Ramon Vega before planting the ball past Espen Baardsen for the second, killer goal. Maine Road went wild.

Berkovic whipped off his shirt and ran to his adoring new army of fans. It was fairytale stuff.

After Paul Robinson had been shown a second yellow card for Watford, Berkovic was substituted to a rapturous standing ovation on 76 minutes – but there was still one more chapter to be written on what was a magical evening for City fans.

With just a few minutes left on the clock, the Blues won a free kick on the edge of the box. If the script was to be followed to the letter, veteran Pearce needed to take it and score one of those trademark howitzers he specialised with so often at Nottingham Forest.

Pearce did step up – and did score with a thunderous free kick – job done and what a way to start your City career. It really was the perfect end to a perfect start for Keegan and his new side.

'It was a tremendous performance,' he said afterwards. 'We didn't get our rewards in the first half – but the lads kept their heads down and the football we played was breathtaking. But I think we can play better.'

They did, too, but the atmosphere and raw passion of that opening game was never bettered.

v Chelsea 6-2

26 November 1977
First Division
Attendance: 34,345

MANCHESTER CITY:	CHELSEA:
Corrigan	Bonetti
Clements	G Wilkins
Donachie	Sparrow
Booth	Britton
Watson	Droy
Barnes	Wicks
Channon	R Wilkins
Tueart	Langley
Kidd	Swain
Hartford	Cooke
Power	Aylott

CITY WENT into this game in patchy form to say the least. Five defeats in the previous eight games had left the Blues slightly adrift of the title chasers having led the table going into October with five wins and two draws from the opening seven games.

It was a time of transition with Joe Royle loaned to Bristol City and making his debut the same day (and scoring all four goals in a 4-1 win for the Ashton Gate side) and Dennis Tueart unhappy at being in and out of the side and on the transfer list. Colin Bell was still absent with the knee injury that had kept him sidelined for the best part of two years, though was back in light training.

Having beaten Manchester United, Liverpool and Arsenal at Maine Road already, the visit of newly-promoted Chelsea represented the perfect opportunity to get the Blues' season back on track.

Oddly, the crowd was well below the 45,000 average with just over 34,000 souls turning up for what was destined to be a cracking afternoon's entertainment, though the Chelsea contingent, tucked away in the top right-hand corner of the Kippax, would soon be wishing they had stayed home and kept warm. It would be a day the Pensioners' full-back Graham Wilkins would remember for a long time, too, and he began his hour of misery by putting through his own net to give City the lead on nine minutes.

Four minutes later the want-away Tueart made it 2-0, with the Blues hardly even breaking into a sweat. It looked for all the world as though City would struggle to have an easier 90 minutes all season, but of course, things rarely pan out that way.

City manager Tony Book urged his side to put Chelsea to the sword from the touchline as it became clear the visitors were there for the taking after a lacklustre opening, but the game was about to turn on its head.

Chelsea somehow dragged themselves into the game and in a surprising twist, first the hapless Wilkins pulled one back for the visitors and on 27 minutes Kenny Clements gave a penalty away that allowed Ian Britton to level the scores at 2-2. Suddenly it was the hosts who looked all at sea and vulnerable at the back.

The crowd showed their displeasure but they needn't have worried as the Blues rallied and re-focused. Book's men were far from finished.

Despite Chelsea's tail wagging and the air of apprehension that had settled over Maine Road, City restored their lead just four minutes later as Tueart scored his second of the afternoon on 31 minutes. Five goals in just over half-an-hour of action – it was bizarre but thoroughly entertaining stuff. And there was plenty more to come.

City began to pummel Chelsea with Asa Hartford and Peter Barnes outstanding, creating chance after chance. It became a matter of time before the Blues struck again rather than if, and, crucially, the sixth goal of the game came just moments before half-time as Paul Power's low drive struck John Sparrow and span towards the opposite corner to keeper Peter Bonetti and the former England custodian could only watch helplessly as the ball trickled over the line to make it 4-2 at the interval.

There was a buzz around the concourses at the break as fans wondered what the final score might possibly be. City had hit Spurs for five the previous May but hadn't hit six in the league at Maine Road for almost exactly ten years when Leicester had been thrashed 6-0 in 1967/68.

The Blues started the second half where they had left the first as the inspirational Barnes continued to terrorise the hapless Wilkins after the break and on 51 minutes the Kippax idol made it 5-2 with a typically classy finish – his fourth of the season – that all-but secured the points for the Blues and piled more misery on the west London side.

In fact, Wilkins, thoroughly fed up with his lot and having chased shadows all afternoon, fouled Barnes repeatedly, eventually giving referee McNally no option but to send him for an early bath. At least his pain was over and it was probably a good move for both teams.

Tueart then completed his hat-trick – his second of the season – on 69 minutes to make it 6-2 and with more than 20 minutes remaining, the City fans urged their team to really rub Chelsea's nose in it, but with both points in the bag, the Blues eased their foot off the gas and there was no more scoring in the remaining time.

As a result, City moved into sixth spot, just five points adrift of Brian Clough's Nottingham Forest and buoyed with confidence. Book's men won their next six successive home games, Bell returned from injury and, for a few weeks, all was well in the world and City seemed strong candidates for a first title in a decade.

Tueart claimed after the game that despite scoring a hat-trick, nothing had changed and he was determined to find a new home. He scored one more hat-trick against Newcastle on Boxing Day before he left for New York Cosmos early in the New Year.

Everton also hit six the day City hammered Chelsea, beating Coventry 6-0. At least the Pensioners clawed back a little defensive pride by holding the Blues to a 0-0 draw in the return fixture at Stamford Bridge, though the memory of that Maine Road drubbing was hardly put to bed in the stalemate.

v Tottenham Hotspur 3-0

2 March 1979
First Division
Attendance: 32,037

MANCHESTER CITY:	TOTTENHAM HOTSPUR:
Corrigan	Kendall
Power	McAllister
Donachie	Holmes
P. Futcher	Lacy
Watson (Deyna 45)	Perryman
Bell	Hoddle
Owen	Galvin
Barnes	Ardiles
Hartford	Armstrong
Kidd	Beavon
Channon	Taylor

MALCOLM ALLISON had been back at Maine Road for a matter of days and already City had been involved in various dramas of one kind or another. Having finished fourth the previous season, Tony Book's side were expected to push on and again challenge Liverpool for the league title and just two defeats in the opening 19 league and cup matches suggested the Blues were again a force to be reckoned with.

But for some reason, from October until February, City couldn't buy a win in the league and embarked on an appalling run that was as mystifying as it was frustrating. Six draws and seven defeats – all by a single goal margin – proved there wasn't a great deal wrong with Book's side, but for whatever reason, they couldn't quite get their act together and were slipping down the table at a steady if not dramatic rate.

There was no doubting the quality of the team which was virtually the same 11 players that had pushed hard for the title for the previous two years, but something wasn't gelling. Whether it was just not getting the rub of the green or something more worrying, something needed to change.

The board, in their infinite wisdom, decided they needed a more charismatic face on the coaching team and decided to bring Malcolm Allison back as Book's right-hand man. The management change meant there was no room for the highly respected first-team City and England coach Bill Taylor, with the popular Scot shown the door at Maine Road – scandalously in many people's eyes.

Another potential problem with Allison's appointment was that his powerful character was bound to make Book's life hard and inevitably there would be questions asked as to who exactly was in charge.

Book had played under Allison just six years earlier and now he was expected to tell his former gaffer what to do – it was a risky move to say the least and undermined Book's authority.

Perhaps that was always the intention of the chairman and his directors who had never lost their fascination in the flamboyant Londoner.

Initially, things seemed to be improving – a 1-1 draw at Leeds United was followed by a home game with Chelsea whom the Blues had already thrashed 4-1 at Stamford Bridge earlier in the campaign and goals from Ron Futcher and Paul Power put City 2-0 up.

It seemed the 13-game winless run was about to end – but the Pensioners, beaten 6-2 at Maine Road 12 months before, scored three times to win the game 3-2 as the crisis deepened.

Worse was to follow when Third Division Shrewsbury Town knocked the Blues out of the FA Cup with a 2-0 win on a frozen Gay Meadow pitch.

With a trip to White Hart Lane next on the agenda, things looked as though they might get worse before they got better. Colin Bell returned to the team for only his second appearance of the season and was employed in a new sweeper role and the game was selected for ITV's *The Big Match*.

Spurs had their own problems having failed to win any of their previous six league matches and their form was indifferent at best so something had to give.

It was clear the first goal was going to lift a huge weight off one team's shoulders and Spurs looked the likelier to break the deadlock. Steve Perryman burst from defence into the Blues half and found himself with just Joe Corrigan to beat after Osvaldo Ardiles's chip was directed into his path but he showed a defender's touch when he nudged the ball just enough for Corrigan to smother the opportunity.

Soon after the hosts had a penalty claim turned down, much to the chagrin of the vast majority of 32,097 fans inside White Hart Lane and within seconds City broke down the other end to take the lead.

Peter Barnes was looking back to his very best and when Gary Owen instinctively played the ball into his path, Perryman clipped Barnes's heels and the referee had no option but to award City a penalty. Brian Kidd stepped up to drive the ball past Mark Kendal and give the Blues a priceless advantage.

There was worse to follow for Spurs when Barnes, in electric form, skipped past three challenges before hammering a left-footed drive past Kendal to make it 2-0 before the break.

Suddenly, City were oozing confidence and appeared to have rediscovered their early season form while the Spurs faithful were vocal in their displeasure, merely adding to the hosts' problems.

Peter Taylor volleyed over from close range before the break and an injury to Dave Watson meant the England defender was substituted at half-time.

Tottenham began the second half brightly but each time Corrigan thwarted their efforts and eventually City regained control.

The goal of the game came on 75 minutes when Owen fed Barnes on the left – the flying winger skipped past McCallister as though he wasn't there, then ghosted past another defender before picking out Mike Channon who made no mistake from close range.

The linesman confused matters by attracting the referee's attention and it seemed the goal may be ruled out, but it was merely to ensure McCallister was booked for trying to impede Barnes in the build-up to the goal.

Barnes and Corrigan had been the difference on the day, one tormenting, jinking and enthralling, the other keeping out everything that had been thrown at him.

As thousands drifted out of White Hart Lane solemnly, City comfortably played out the final moments to claim a fine victory. It proved something of a false dawn as the Blues went down by the same scoreline in the Manchester derby a week later at Maine Road.

34

v Manchester United 4-0

15 November 1969
First Division
Attendance: 63,013

MANCHESTER CITY:	MANCHESTER UNITED:
Corrigan	Stepney
Book	Brennan
Pardoe (Heslop)	Dunne
Doyle	Burns
Booth	Ure
Oakes	Sadler
Summerbee	Sartori (Kidd)
Bell	Best
Lee	Charlton
Young	Law
Bowyer	Aston

THEY CALLED it one of the most one-sided derby matches ever – a football massacre, in fact – and the majority of the massive 63,000 crowd remembered it for many years, with plenty of good reason.

The news reports commented on the 'vast gulf between two ill-matched sides' – manna from heaven for all the Blues who particularly enjoyed rubbing their neighbours' noses in the mud.

City went into the match having failed to beat United at Maine Road since September 1959, but in good form in the league having lost just one of their previous 13 games – winning eight of them. There was a feeling that if that dismal run was to finally end, there would be no better chance than this.

Both sides were still attempting to get back on the rails having both endured mediocre 1968/69 campaigns while, in City's case, defending the title, and in United's, the European Cup.

While the Blues were riding high, the Reds were clearly going through something of a transitional period. In truth, the monumental efforts both teams had put into making each club the pride of the city for obvious reasons, though neither, of course, would say as much.

City's slow start to the campaign during which they had won two of their opening eight matches meant they probably wouldn't be successful in their bid to lift a second title in three years, though the possibility was still there. The campaign before had flopped due to an exhausting post-season trip to the USA which lasted some six weeks into the middle of June.

With the teams due to meet again in a two-legged League Cup semi-final just a few weeks later, it was important to gain an edge to take into those games and it was United who came desperately close to opening the scoring in the first minute, with Denis Law just failing to connect with John Aston's inviting ball across the box. Had that gone in, who knows which way the game might have swung.

But City received all the incentive to go for the Reds' throats when a horrific tackle by George Best left Glyn Pardoe with a broken leg and incensed the City players.

Mike Doyle, cousin and close friend of Pardoe, attempted to throttle Best who, in fairness, rarely attracted the attention of the referee. When the melee had calmed down and Pardoe had been rushed to hospital, the pumped up Blues tore into United.

The hosts effortlessly slipped up a gear from that moment on, though United resisted initially, and it wasn't until the 38th minute that the hosts finally went in front.

The ever graceful Neil Young had been fairly quiet up to that point, but when he received the ball within sight of goal, he feigned to cross but instead sent in a wicked curling drive that totally fooled Alex Stepney and flew into the back of the net – his fifth of the campaign, all of which had been scored at Maine Road.

The relief was palpable and with their tails up, Joe Mercer's men set about dismantling the European champions as the battle for Manchester supremacy continued.

Still, with just one goal separating the sides at the break, the Reds could have been forgiven for thinking they had a good shot at clawing their way back into the match, but ten minutes after half-time the peerless Colin Bell doubled City's advantage to make it 2-0 with his eighth of the season, putting him one ahead of Francis Lee.

United's talismanic trio of Bobby Charlton, Law and George Best were powerless to prevent the continued tidal wave of attacks, led by man of the match Bell, and when the Blues went 3-0 up courtesy of an own goal, the

Kippax began to enjoy the occasion, safe in the knowledge that there was no way back for Sir Matt Busby's boys.

The City fans tormented their opposites who, by then, were praying for the exit gates to be opened early.

Mike Summerbee, Lee, Young and Bell had attacked from the front relentlessly with a mixture of flair and aggression and United had been overwhelmed. In short, the Blues had been far more up for the game than the Reds.

Alan Oakes, Glyn Pardoe, Tony Book and, of course, Mike Doyle, played like men inspired and nobody was about to take their foot off the gas, least of all the majestic Bell who scrambled home a fourth on 89 minutes to send Maine Road into ecstasy and complete United's nightmarish afternoon.

City had shown championship class and looked capable of really kicking on from that point.

Malcolm Allison had instilled a real belief within his troops that United were nothing to be scared of – he had told them to go out prior to derbies at Old Trafford and walk in front of the Stretford End, effectively taking the fear away and the move paid instant dividends with successive wins at United in 1968 and 1969 and, once again, that helped the Blues triumph again a few weeks later, beating the Reds 2-1 in the first leg of the League Cup semi-final and drawing 2-2 in the return.

Oddly, with many expecting City to make a genuine challenge for the title following the demolition derby, Mercer's side won just one of their next 12 games and would actually finish below United in the table.

On the plus side, City completed the double over United and won the League Cup against West Brom a few months later. And they won the European Cup Winners' Cup, too. It wasn't such a bad season after all.

v Aston Villa 4-1

24 August 1977
First Division
Attendance: 40,121

MANCHESTER CITY:	ASTON VILLA:
Corrigan	Rimmer
Clements	Gregory
Donachie	Smith
Doyle	Phillips
Watson	McNaught
Booth	Mortimer
Kidd	Deehan
Channon	Little
Royle	Gray
Hartford	Cropley
Tueart	Carrodus

C ITY HAD missed out on the 1976/77 title by a solitary point to Liverpool and in doing so, changed the club's future completely over the next 20 years – though nobody knew as much at the time.

Had the Blues taken top spot, who knows how they would have fared in the European Cup. They may have ducked out in the first round – no lucrative group stages back in the 1970s – or they might have gone on to win it.

One thing was for sure, there was enough talent in Tony Book's side to have achieved anything they wanted to, with a little rub of the green – and a fit Colin Bell.

As with most teams who had achieved the right blend of talent and experience, only minor maintenance was needed for the new campaign and, hopefully, it would be the difference between finishing second and first.

England striker Mike Channon was the only player to be added to the side, with the arm-swinging signing from Southampton costing a club record fee of £300,000.

City were again among the favourites for the title, as were their opponents on this day, Aston Villa.

Wearing the iconic white shirts with a black and red diagonal slash across, the Blues went into the second game of the 1977/78 campaign on the back of a disappointing 0-0 draw at home to Leicester City. Gary Owen was dropped in favour of Brian Kidd and the teams ran out to a packed Villa Park on a warm, bright evening in the Midlands.

This was the second meeting between the clubs in five games with Villa holding City 1-1 in the same fixture at the back end of the previous campaign.

Former Blues manager Ron Saunders was now in charge at Villa and, ironically, his last act as City boss had been to sign Dennis Tueart from Sunderland and it's a fair bet he wished he had never even heard of Tueart by the time this game had finished.

Villa roared out of the blocks, intent on giving a noisy, partisan crowd exactly what they wanted and with just four minutes gone, John Deehan put the ball past Joe Corrigan to put the hosts ahead. It was just the start Book didn't want. Yet just two minutes later, it was the travelling supporters going wild as Tommy Booth headed home powerfully from a corner to level the scores at the Holte End.

It had been an exhilarating start to the match and the next goal would be crucial – and both teams went at each other hammer and tongs looking for it.

Villa should have re-taken the lead when Alex Cropley was twice presented with opportunities to put the hosts back in front within the space of four minutes but each time he fluffed his lines.

Whether that put seeds of doubt into the Villa players' minds that perhaps it might not be their night, particularly after their blistering start, is unknown, but on 28 minutes, Tueart scored his first of the night, recreating his spectacular overhead League Cup Final winner.

Mike Doyle launched a huge throw into the box towards Channon who jumped but seemed to be pushed as he went up. The ball sailed over both his and the defender's head and bounced once before Tueart acrobatically bicycle-kicked a superb goal with Rimmer stunned in goal.

It was typical Tueart – inventive improvisation that was both deadly and opportunistic – no wonder he was the idol of thousands of kids.

City pressed for a third and Villa tried to build up a head of steam, but there was an air of calm about the Blues' play suggesting they were in command of proceedings.

There were no further goals in the first period and the players were greeted by a torrential downpour after the break, with Book asking for 'more of the same' from his players.

City looked slick, their passing was smooth and incisive and Villa's threat was occasional but not constant and when they did break through, Corrigan was at his best.

Booth, Doyle and Dave Watson were magnificent at the back and the home team's will began to weaken as it became clear the Blues repelled everything they could throw at them.

Despite this, the result was far from clear cut and the travelling 4,000 or so from Manchester were left biting their nails, nerves typically frayed, as the clocked ticked towards the final five minutes.

City upped the tempo a fraction and reaped their rewards when, on 84 minutes, Tueart took advantage of some hesitant defending to make it 3-1 with a smart finish past Rimmer.

The best was yet to come three minutes later as Tueart out-did himself with the goal of the night.

With Villa accepting their fate, the City winger/striker raced on to Kenny Clements's long clearance and left his marker chasing shadows.

As former Manchester United keeper Rimmer ran towards the edge of the box, Tueart calmly dinked the ball and into the net from 25 yards to complete his hat-trick – his first away from Maine Road – and put the seal on an emphatic 4-1 win.

It had been a superb personal performance by the England forward and a fantastic night for City.

Tueart went on to score two more hat-tricks that season before heading off to play for New York Cosmos in the embryonic North American Soccer League.

The Blues would, in his absence, win just two of their remaining seven league games to finish in fourth place. Had he stayed, who knows what might have happened.

MANCHESTER CITY:	WOLVERHAMPTON WANDERERS:
Corrigan	Parkes
Book	Shaw
Donachie	Parkin
Doyle	Sunderland
Booth	Munro
Oakes	McAlle
Summerbee (Hill 60)	McCalliog
Bell	Hibbitt
Davies	Richards
Lee	Dougan
Towers	Wagstaffe

GOING INTO game 29 of the 1971/72 campaign, City had lost only four times all season. The defeats came against sides the Blues traditionally struggled against – Leeds United (twice), Derby County and Wolverhampton Wanderers with the latter the opponents on a dull, cold Saturday afternoon at Maine Road.

The teams had met at Molineux back in August and the Black Country men had triumphed 2-1.

A fortnight later the Blues gained revenge as they edged a seven-goal thriller in a League Cup second round clash at Maine Road, so the hardy souls who shivered away on the Kippax for this game at least felt there was a chance of an entertaining afternoon ahead.

Franny Lee was in white hot form and had already bagged 20 goals going into this match – including a strike in each game against Bill McGarry's Wolves – and the little and large partnership with Wyn Davies was proving irresistible.

Tony Towers was in the form of his life and Mercer only changed his starting line-up when absolutely necessary, much like the 1967/68 championship season when the team-sheet only changed through injury or suspension and there was a real belief the Blues could bring the title back to Maine Road again.

Former Kippax idol Dave Wagstaffe made a welcome return in the gold and black of Wolves, who themselves were in sparkling form and making a determined surge up the First Division table.

With City level with leaders Leeds and Wolves knowing a victory would put them just two points behind the Blues, the scene was set for a cracking afternoon's football and City, who had already taken 21 points from a possible 26 at home, immediately took the game to the visitors.

With Stan Gibson's pitch reduced to a cabbage patch with the odd blade of grass here and there, the ball was never going to move around the surface smoothly and so both teams adopted a more direct approach than usual.

The Blues stole a march after just five minutes when Tommy Booth rose to head home and put his team 1-0 up and on 24 minutes Lee scored his 21st of the season to seemingly put the hosts in the box-seat.

But as dangerous as City were, there was a frailty about the home defence that Wolves began to exploit. Joe Corrigan didn't seem to be at the races at that time as he struggled with his weight and his defenders were hardly watertight – it was seven games since they collectively kept a clean sheet – and on 34 minutes, the prolific John Richards pulled a goal back.

City were stirred into a quick response and within six minutes Towers had restored the Blues' two-goal advantage to make it 3-1 – a lead they took into the half-time break.

Yet whatever Mercer and Malcolm Allison said to the team as they sipped their tea in the dressing room, it didn't work immediately as the dangerous Richards again brought Wolves back into the game with his second of the afternoon coming just six minutes after the re-start.

It was proving an absorbing clash, perhaps even more so because the Blues were aware that if results went their way, they would go into February as the league leaders.

On the hour, the impressive Mike Summerbee limped off and substitute Freddie Hill climbed off the bench for his first appearance of the season – and it was Hill who definitively changed the sway of the game, adding a new dimension to City's midfield that had strangely lacked spark, mainly due to Colin Bell having a rare off-day – though his off-days were the equivalent of an average player's high.

The next goal was going to be critical. If it went the way of City, surely there would be no way back for the visitors. If Wolves levelled, however, they would fancy themselves to go on and clinch both points having already scored three times at Maine Road once that season.

Fortunately, super-sub Hill proved to be the catalyst for the Blues to push on and eventually win in a canter.

His back-headed flick from Bell's cross landed perfectly for Lee to crack home City's fourth just past the hour-mark, allowing a nervy Maine Road to settle and enjoy the last third of the game, and Lee provided the perfect coup de grace by completing his hat-trick with two minutes to go.

With 14 goals spread over two meetings between these two clubs, this was clearly a fixture that produced value for money at the turnstile!

With a 5-2 home win in the bank and a defeat for leaders Leeds United, City smoothly moved two points clear at the top with just 14 games to go.

Even during a patchy performance they had proved they had sufficient gears to ease past tricky opposition – the title beckoned ... at least until Malcolm Allison decided on bringing Rodney Marsh to Maine Road for the final few furlongs which seemed to affect the balance of the team.

Towers made way for the mercurial Marsh and the goals began to dry up meaning that 37-year-old Brian Clough instead guided his Derby County side to the title by a solitary point.

It really had been City's title for the taking but four successive defeats in March meant the Blues eventually finished fourth – one of three teams a point behind Derby.

As for Wolves, they finished in mid-table and reached the UEFA Cup final where they lost 3-2 over two legs against Tottenham Hotspur.

v SK Lierse **5-0**

37

26 November 1969
European Cup Winners' Cup second round second leg
Attendance: 26,486

MANCHESTER CITY:	SK LIERSE:
Mulhearn	Engelen
Book	Van den Eynde
Pardoe	Boogaerts
Doyle	Michielsens (Laeremans 77)
Booth	Mertens
Oakes	Willems
Summerbee (Hill)	Van Opstal
Bell	Janssens
Bowyer (Towers)	De Ceulaer
Lee	Denul
Jeffries	Min (Put 65)

THE NOW defunct European Cup Winners' Cup consisted of just 32 clubs when the Blues entered the competition as FA Cup holders in the 1969/70 season. Four aggregate victories would send two clubs all the way to the final in Vienna, though the pedigree of the teams competing was obviously high with the accent very much on quality over quantity.

Briefly, the Cup Winners' Cup was a tournament solely for teams who had won domestic competitions across Europe with England's only representatives being the FA Cup holders (winning the League Cup didn't merit European qualification at the time).

Rangers, Ards and Cardiff City were the other British entrants, though all three would be eliminated by the third round.

Koninklijke Lierse Sportkring – better known as SK Lierse – were a part-time outfit from Belgium who weren't expected to progress too far in the competition, but they had seen off Cypriot side APOEL in the previous round, winning the home leg 10-1 and 1-0 in Cyprus so they were no mugs.

They had won the Belgian Cup for the first time to qualify for the competition, so this was their first foray into European competition for almost a decade having gone down 5-0 to Barcelona in their first attempt.

Still, City eased through the first leg with a 3-0 win at the Herman Vanderpoortenstadion, making the return game at Maine Road seemingly nothing more than a formality; however the opening exchanges proved to be anything but.

City were a long way from their best in the league, but still came into the game unbeaten in 13 games in all competitions.

Six wins and three draws had propelled the team towards the top of the table but there was still something missing from the team that had won the title with such swagger just a couple of years earlier.

It seemed the Blues could turn on the style like a tap, but the occasions were becoming less frequent. As with the campaign before, the cup competitions offered salvation and a chance to continue the flow of silverware the fans were starting to become accustomed to.

Lierse sensed that their only hope of a miraculous turnaround was to grasp the game by the throat and give everything in the opening exchanges in the hope they could rattle the hosts, who would be expecting gentle progression into the next round.

The Belgians came at City like tigers and should have been 2-0 up inside 15 minutes, such was their dominance. Had they taken their chances, the Blues just might have been on the end of one of the most dramatic comebacks in the history of European club competition.

Lierse striker De Nul was causing no end of problems and had one effort scrambled off the line and he then hit the post with a snap shot out of nothing, with Ken Mulhearn well beaten.

The visitors had clearly understood their manager's instructions to throw caution to the wind and see where it took them and their brave approach earned the respect of a half-full Maine Road.

Of course, what many of the crowd were wondering – perhaps none more so than the tiny contingent from Belgium – was why they hadn't adopted a similar approach in the first leg. If they had, backed by 19,000 passionate home fans, they may have arrived in Manchester with a fighting chance. Freezing conditions had left the pitch rock hard and the Blues were finding it difficult to get the ball on the ground and play their natural passing game but, in true ballet on ice style, a change of footwear (this time at the break), would prove the undoing of their opponents.

Lierse had done well to get to the break with the score still 0-0. As each minute passed, their chances diminished but they had at least won a little pride back. Their unrewarded efforts, however, quickly took their toll and when City finally did shift up a gear, the floodgates quickly opened.

Just three minutes after the re-start, Mike Summerbee blasted City ahead, ending any lingering hopes Lierse might have entertained and from then on, the Blues dominated with Colin Bell and Francis Lee particularly impressive, adding a goal each in quick succession to make it three goals in 12 minutes.

Youngster Derek Jeffries was making a good impression with his intelligent passing and technique standing out, but it was Bell and Lee who completed the rout, each scoring another goal to give City a 5-0 win on the night and 8-0 aggregate overall – a club record which still stood at the time of writing.

Lierse headed back to Belgium chastised, but with their heads held high having played their part in the European night.

While City went on to win the competition, Lierse learned from their experience and two years later, a similar situation arose that is worth mentioning here for those who thought they never really had a chance of overturning the first leg deficit.

In 1971, Lierse again faced English opposition in the UEFA Cup first round in the form of the then-dominant Leeds United.

The first leg in Belgium went to form and the Yorkshire side eased home 2-0. It had been expected but Lierse again had not given up hope and, as they had against City two years earlier, they started at a more measured pace against what was very much a Leeds reserve team.

Two goals just before half-time stunned the Elland Road faithful and two more after the break gave Lierse a famous 4-0 victory and a 4-2 aggregate win. The Blues had treated the opposition with greater respect and triumphed while Leeds had not.

v Scunthorpe United 8-1

26 December 1963
Second Division
Attendance: 26,365

MANCHESTER CITY:	SCUNTHORPE UNITED:
Dowd	Jones
Betts	Hemstead
Sear	Brownsword
Kennedy	Gibson
Wood	Horstead
Oakes	Gannon
Young	Crwford
Gray	Hodgson
Murray	Kirkman
Kevan	Lawther
Wagstaffe	Wilson

THE BLUES went into the 1963/64 season having been relegated the season before, so ending a proud 12-year stay in the top flight for Les McDowall's side. Despite ending Tottenham's title hopes with a 1-0 win at Maine Road three games before the end of a miserable campaign, a 1-1 draw with Manchester United sent City tumbling out of the top flight for the first time since 1951 and the final match against West Ham – a 6-1 thrashing – added insult to injury for such a proud club.

Even more galling to supporters was the fact that the point United took at Maine Road ensured their survival while the Blues and Leyton Orient, who had been relegated a month earlier, went down.

McDowall left the club after an amazing 13 years in charge with the embarrassing manner of the defeat at Upton Park his final act as boss. City's goals conceded tally had reached 102 so there was work aplenty for the new manager.

George Poyser, McDowall's number two for the past six years, was given the chance to manage City and the decision was not an unpopular one with players or supporters.

Poyser showed astuteness in the transfer market, too, signing Derek Kevan from Chelsea as well as adding Jimmy Murray from his former club Wolves in November.

As they also had Matt Gray, plus Neil Young and Dave Wagstaffe on the flanks, the Blues possessed one of the most lethal attacks in the division and were tipped by many to make a quick return to the top league, though with the likes of Leeds United and Sunderland, both of whom narrowly missed out on promotion the previous season, it was going to be a tough ask.

The first half of the campaign would be one of few highs, one of which was a 3-2 win over Leeds at Maine Road in front of a crowd approaching 30,000.

The Blues had started promisingly with seven points from a possible ten and Kevan proved an instant success with five goals in five games, but just one win in the next nine saw Poyser's side plummet down the table while both Leeds and Sunderland kicked on, opening up a gap of several points.

Jimmy Murray scored on his debut for City in a 4-2 defeat at Southampton and another loss, this time away to Newcastle United, had the pundits writing off the Blues' hopes of promotion with still one game in November to play and rightly so – six wins, five draws and seven defeats as the halfway mark approached meant just 17 points had been amassed from a possible 36.

The Blues needed a shot in the arm and the arrival of the prolific Murray proved to be that and more. Murray settled in quickly and soon found a kindred spirit in strike partner Kevan.

City found renewed hope after a 5-2 home win over Huddersfield Town and that was followed with a 2-0 win away to Leyton Orient.

As the festive programme approached, the Blues took a useful point in a 2-2 draw at Portsmouth and followed it up with their last game before Christmas in emphatic style – a 6-1 victory over a decent Rotherham United team meant the home match in the double-header against struggling Scunthorpe United on Boxing Day could be another chance for the Blues to add to their impressive goals tally.

Since Murray's arrival, City had scored 18 goals in just six games and Murray had helped himself to eight of them – a fantastic return – and Kevan had helped himself to another seven.

As the country settled down for their Christmas Day dinner, Poyser enjoyed a bottle of beer and puffed away on his beloved pipe as he plotted the downfall of The Iron and a chilly Maine Road opened its gates the following day for an expectant crowd of 26,365 – the second highest of the season.

But for 40 minutes, Scunthorpe gave as good as they got, keeping the country's most prolific strike force at bay and almost holding out for a more than respectable goalless first period.

When, however, the Lincolnshire outfit finally succumbed to the constant home attacks, inevitably it was Murray who opened the scoring with a clinical finish just before the break.

Whatever Poyser said to his slightly mis-firing troops during the half-time break certainly worked as the Blues shifted up several gears thereafter and for the first time since the Second World War, City bagged seven goals in one half at an average of one goal every six and a half minutes.

Murray was unstoppable, completing his second successive hat-trick – in fact his second treble in five days – and Matt Gray also hit a treble to double his haul for the season in one fell swoop.

Kevan wasn't to be left out, scoring the other two in the 8-1 victory that firmly established the Blues as promotion hopefuls once again – not to mention sending the punters home with a bucket-load of optimism.

Two days later the exact same starting 11 beat a thoroughly demoralised Scunthorpe 4-2 at the Old Showground with Murray scoring two more to take his tally to 13 in eight games, making him the most in-form striker in the country.

With 27 goals in six games, Poyser's side were in white-hot form going into their top-of-the-table clashes with Leeds and Sunderland in the New Year. Unfortunately, the Blues found their promotion rivals an altogether different proposition, losing 1-0 to Leeds and 3-0 at home to the Black Cats.

In fact, failure to win any of the next seven games meant the promotion dream was effectively over by mid-February and the Blues eventually finished sixth with Leeds and Sunderland winning promotion to the top flight. Still, what a Christmas.

v Gornik Zabrze 3-1

31 March 1971
European Cup Winners' Cup third round replay
Attendance: 12,100

MANCHESTER CITY:	GORNIK ZABRZE:
Healey	Kostka
Connor	Wrazy (Olek 65)
Towers	Oslizlo
Doyle	Latocha
Booth	Gorgon
Donachie	Szoltysik
Jeffries	Deja
Bell	Skowronek
Lee	Banas
Young	Lubanski
Hill	Szarynsli (Wilim 46)

I N THE league, City couldn't buy a goal and were in the middle of an atrocious run. One strike in eight games and seven blanks meant Joe Mercer's side were well out of the title race and the First Division was proving an extremely tight league with everyone seemingly able to beat each other.

Having ducked out of the FA Cup and League Cup, the European Cup Winners' Cup represented the only hope of a fourth successive season of landing silverware, but with the City strikers mis-firing badly, it was hard to see where the goals would come from. Whether it was the end of an era or just a lack of confidence, the Blues were in desperate need of a pick-me-up.

The path to the third round had not been without its own dramas, either. City had drawn Northern Irish part-timers Linfield and just about edged through a particularly hairy tie, winning 1-0 at Maine Road but losing 2-1 in a hostile environment in Belfast where police were called to quell crowd disturbances behind Joe Corrigan's goal.

It got so bad Linfield boss Billy Bingham was forced to make a personal appeal for calm. Clearly ruffled, City went down 2-1 but edged through on the away goals rule.

Hungarian side Honved, once the employers of the great Ferenc Puskas and the side that provided the nucleus of the famous 'Mighty Magyars' back in the 1950s, proved no less of a thorn, with only Franny Lee's goal in Budapest giving the Blues a narrow 1-0 lead in the first leg. Lee was again on target in the return as he and Bell helped City to a 2-0 win, though it hadn't been as comfortable as it perhaps should have been.

But as defending champions, the Blues felt a special affinity with this competition. Then came a reminder of that rain-soaked evening in Vienna when City pulled old foes Gornik Zabrze out of the hat in the last eight for a repeat of the 1970 Cup Winners' Cup Final with the Poles determined to avenge the defeat in Vienna 12 months before.

The first leg for the out-of-sorts Blues was in Poland and with 100,000 fanatical supporters screaming for their heroes on an icy, frozen pitch, the hosts won 2-0 with two well-worked goals.

Mike Doyle, sensing the euphoria around the stadium at the final whistle, urged his team-mates to copy his mock celebrations as though the result had in fact been a moral victory for the Blues. It worked like a charm as a cacophony of noise gradually muted.

Despite the odds being stacked against them, the mind games worked and City triumphed 2-0 at Maine Road with goals from Mike Doyle and Ian Mellor levelling the aggregate score, but with no penalties to settle the tie, a replay in Copenhagen was organised a week later. Odd, but it's how things were decided back then.

It was proving to be an expensive round for the loyal supporters who travelled over to Denmark to form part of the 12,100 crowd that also included many curious locals, keen to watch a re-enactment of one of European football's major finals on their own doorstep.

Just 11 months earlier the Blues had faced Gornik on neutral soil in Austria and won through – and now the teams again locked horns for the right to face Chelsea in the semi-final.

Mercer's team settled in to the unfamiliar surroundings far quicker than Gornik did and with Doyle marauding forward and roughing up keeper Kostlea, Gornik looked vulnerable at the back and the first goal was born out of apprehension from the Polish custodian.

Neil Young, with just one league goal all season, sent in a powerful drive that Kostlea could only deflect downwards and up into the roof of the net, giving the Blues a 1-0 lead.

Gornik looked bereft of ideas and fell further behind from a set-piece when the impressive and unmarked Tommy Booth headed home the second at the far post – for what looked a killer second goal for City.

Gornik did rally briefly after the break and the dangerous Wlodzimierz Lubanski finally pulled one back on 57 minutes, showing the predatory instincts that would bag him 24 goals in 34 games that season to make it 2-1, and only a fantastic save by Ronnie Healey stopped Gornik levelling two minutes later.

Fortunately, City still had plenty in reserve and when Colin Bell picked the ball up some 50 yards from goal, there seemed little threat to the Gornik defence, but Nijinsky then burst forward and glided past five players as though they weren't there before firing a low drive in that was parried by the keeper and tapped home by Franny Lee for a decisive third on 65 minutes.

There was no further scoring and Mercer's side eased through 3-1 to book a two-legged semi-final with Chelsea a fortnight later.

Gornik boss Ferenc Suzousa said afterwards, 'I hold my hands up, Manchester City were a mile better than us tonight. Now I wish them luck in their quest to retain the trophy.'

Unfortunately, injuries meant the first leg at Stamford Bridge was always going to be difficult and though City lost only 1-0, the second leg again showed the striking deficiencies of the Blues as they again lost 1-0 to exit the competition and complete a largely miserable season with no silverware to add to the trophy cabinet.

As a footnote, Chelsea went on to play Real Madrid in the final in Athens and led 1-0 until the Spaniards equalised in the 90th minute. Two days later, Chelsea triumphed 2-1 over Madrid so the trophy at least remained in England, though sadly not in Manchester.

v Blackburn Rovers 6-0

17 September 1983
Second Division
Attendance: 25,443

MANCHESTER CITY:	BLACKBURN ROVERS:
Williams	O'Keefe
Ranson	Branagan
May	Rathbone
Bond	Randell (Patterson)
Power	Keeley
Caton	Fazackerley
McNab	Miller
Reid	Lowey
Baker	Thompson
Tolmie	Garner
Parlane (Davidson)	Hamilton

AFTER SUFFERING relegation on the final day of the 1982/83 campaign, the Blues had to hit the ground running if they were to return to the top flight at the first attempt. City's last game outside the First Division had been a 0-0 draw with Southampton back in May 1966 and the fixture list for the 1983/84 campaign produced a myriad of clubs City hadn't faced in league action for many years.

No longer were the Blues destined for Anfield, Old Trafford, Highbury and Villa Park – it was time to dust off the A to Z as City had a completely new itinerary with destinations such as Cardiff City's Ninian Park, Grimsby Town's Blundell Park, Charlton Athletic's The Valley, Carlisle United's Brunton Park and Cambridge United's Abbey Stadium.

All held novelty value, but little else. For a club City's size, the need to win promotion at the first time of asking was critical. The second tier of English football was littered with 'sleeping giants' who were closer to being comatose after numerous failed attempts to regain their lofty status and the Blues couldn't afford to join the catatonics.

Any league that included Chelsea, Leeds and Newcastle United was going to be tough to escape from, but new manager Billy McNeill was well aware of the task ahead and had recruited players he knew well – mostly fellow Scots – who he felt could do a decent job.

There was hardly any transfer kitty to speak of, so Neil McNab, Jim Tolmie and Derek Parlane were all brought in for under £150,000 combined, while the big earning Joe Corrigan, Dennis Tueart, David Cross and Asa Hartford had all moved on to pastures new.

McNeill's new-look team had begun the season with a 2-0 win at Crystal Palace but then lost 2-1 at Cardiff just two days later. A thrilling 3-2 victory over Barnsley suggested the Parlane/Tolmie partnership could be particularly fruitful with the pair already responsible for five of the six goals scored so far. A frustrating 0-0 draw with Fulham was then followed by a 2-1 win at Portsmouth – Tolmie and Parlane again scoring the goals – meaning that the Blues ran out at Maine Road to face Blackburn Rovers handily placed in fourth position.

Rovers had only lost one of their opening five games and had conceded just five goals in the process so anything but an easy ride was expected by the 25,443 crowd – the third highest in the country that day, underling the pull and potential of the Blues, no matter what their status was.

City wore a Saab-sponsored all-sky blue kit while Rovers, backed by around 1,000 travelling fans, were all in yellow.

With the sun shining and the Kippax in good voice, the Blues were quick to force Rovers on to the back foot and with just 11 minutes on the clock, Andy May put City ahead with his second goal of the campaign but there was much more to come.

On 27 minutes, City went 2-0 up thanks to a cracking drive from Parlane who was quickly becoming a crowd favourite and a bargain in the process. The tall former Leeds United, Rangers and Scotland striker didn't do a great deal outside of the box, but in it, he looked a true predator and though there was concern when he hobbled off for treatment on 35 minutes, he returned to put the game beyond doubt on 41 minutes when he made it 3-0 from close range.

City, by now rampant, had no answer. Tolmie and Parlane looked as though they had been playing alongside each other for years and the pair continued their scoring exploits after the break, with Parlane completing a thoroughly deserved 23-minute hat-trick on 50 minutes and Tolmie adding a fifth on 52 meaning they had now scored 11 of City's 13 goals so far that season.

With such a massive lead achieved before the hour, it also begged the question of how many goals the Blues might score that day. McNeill must have been chuffed that his gamble on the pint-sized Tolmie was paying off.

He had paid Belgian side Lokeren just £30,000 to secure his services and this after Tolmie had failed to score in 18 appearances! McNeill must have seen something in the diminutive forward's play during his time with Morton that had clearly stuck in his head.

The 12-times capped Parlane was less of a risk, even aged 30, though his record at previous club Leeds United averaged just one goal in every five matches.

If McNeill was to guide City back to the First Division, he would need Parlane and Tolmie to continue their rich vein of form throughout the season. His gamble thus far was clearly paying off but it had to continue throughout the season.

The Blues still had time to really rub Blackburn's noses in the mud with former Southampton midfielder Graham Baker adding a sixth before full-time.

It was City's biggest home win since Leyton Orient had been beaten by the same score in August 1964 and it pushed them into second place in the table, a point behind leaders Sheffield Wednesday.

Three successive league wins followed to put McNeill's men at the division's summit, but the squad's frailties emerged as the months passed by and despite the Tolmie/Parlane partnership yielding a total of 34 goals, City finished in fourth position, ten points adrift of third-placed Newcastle.

McNeill went back to the drawing board and though Tolmie and Parlane wouldn't rekindle the magical scoring form the season after, both had proved what great strikers they could be – given the right foil, conditions and belief.

v Burnley 5-1

29 December 2001
First Division
Attendance: 34,250

MANCHESTER CITY:	BURNLEY:
Nash	Michopoulos
Howey	West (Papadopoulos 71)
Wiekens (Dunne 21)	Cox
Mettomo	Gnohere
Edghill (Wright-Phillips 80)	Briscoe
Benarbia	Little
Berkovic	Ball
Horlock	Grant
Tiatto	A. Moore
Wanchope	Taylor
Goater (Huckerby 65)	I. Moore (Ellis 81)

KEVIN KEEGAN had certainly made an impact at Maine Road but there was still plenty of work to do. Anyone who imagined City would waltz away with the second tier title were mistaken – at least for the first part of the season when the Blues were once again everybody's cup final.

Burnley were the surprise package of the 2001/02 campaign and arrived at Maine Road for the final game of 2001 four points clear of second-placed City at the top of the First Division.

The Blues were under pressure, too, from a clutch of clubs determined to hunt them down in any way possible – there were six clubs within four points in what was proving a highly-competitive campaign.

City had to go into the New Year on a high and the thought of ending the day seven points behind the Clarets was not even entertained.

Having only managed to draw their previous home game 0-0 against third-placed West Brom, nothing less than a win would satisfy the capacity Maine Road crowd, with just over 2,000 travelling Burnley fans eager for their team to avenge a 4-2 defeat by City back in August – their only defeat at Turf Moor so far.

Keegan demanded that his team go out and attack, play with freedom and believe in their own ability, and with the talismanic talents of Ali

Benarbia and Eyal Berkovic scheming behind strikers Shaun Goater and Paulo Wanchope, he knew his instructions would be carried out to the letter.

'The Goat', with 22 goals under his belt already, was going through something of a lean patch by his standards and was goalless in the past four games, while his strike partner Wanchope hadn't scored for three months, though a knee problem accounted for most of that time.

Skipper Stuart Pearce was still missing through injury and Shaun Wright-Phillips was on the bench, otherwise City were at full strength. If the Clarets thought they were going to come to Maine Road and teach their bigger city cousins a lesson, they were soon dismissed as the hosts set about their business.

The Blues tore into Burnley straight from the kick-off and with just two minutes gone Goater found space and delivered a low cross into the six-yard box where Wanchope slid the ball past Nick Michopoulos and into the net. It was the perfect start and a message to the division that the leaders may be Burnley, but the best team in the division were City.

But this was only the start of what would prove to be an extraordinary afternoon.

Gerard Wiekens picked up an injury on 21 minutes and was replaced by Richard Dunne, but the visitors were not leading the table by luck. They came into the game having won six out of their last seven matches and were unbeaten in their last ten. Their neat interplay saw them have plenty of possession without ever really threatening Carlo Nash's goal – until a controversial penalty was awarded for the Clarets midway through the half.

Glenn Little stepped up only to see his shot saved by Nash and not long after, Burnley had another great chance to equalise when Kevin Ball saw his header cleared off the line by Kevin Horlock, but that was as good as it got in the first 45.

Wanchope raced clear thanks to a sublime Benarbia through ball and finished clinically with a low drive past Michopoulos to make it 2-0 and send the home fans wild. Some of the Blues' passing was a joy to watch and as the City fans taunted the away section banked to the right of the North Stand, the Blues went 3-0 up.

This time Wanchope and Goater combined superbly to lay off a chance for Berkovic on the edge of the box and the Israeli cracked home a fantastic shot to ensure the points were City's even with almost an hour still to play, but there still more to come.

Berkovic and Benarbia were at their brilliant best and the Clarets were simply being outclassed and on 44 minutes, City sent out a message that would send a shudder down the rest of the division's spine.

Berkovic again slipped the ball perfectly through to Wanchope and the Costa Rican, in a carbon copy of his second goal, calmly slipped the ball past Michopoulos after a passage of play the Burnley defence weren't particularly proud of, to make it 4-0 at the break.

Maine Road stood as one to applaud the team off the field while Burnley's fans must have feared a cricket score, not to mention the severe dent in their team's promotion hopes.

As so often happens though, the second half was something of an anti-climax, with the visitors settling for damage limitation and the Blues playing pretty patterns but relaxed in the knowledge the job was as good as done.

Ian Moore reminded the Blues they couldn't take their foot too far off the gas with a goal on 60 minutes to make it 4-1, but there was never going to be a chance of a comeback.

Keegan, knowing the possibility that goal difference could play a major role in the final table of the campaign, sent on substitute Darren Huckerby and it was the former Coventry City man who had the last word, running on to Berkovic's sublime pass to finish clinically and complete an impressive 5-1 victory.

A 3-1 win at Sheffield United three days later put City top while Burnley's confidence was so shattered they would win just one of their next seven league games and just two of their next 11.

The Blues romped to the title but Burnley didn't even make the play-offs, finishing seventh.

v Gillingham 2-2

30 May 1999
Second Division play-off final, Wembley Stadium
Attendance: 76,935

MANCHESTER CITY:	GILLINGHAM:
Weaver	Bartram
Crooks (G Taylor 85)	M Patterson (Hodge 105)
Edghill	Butters
Wiekens	Ashby
Morrison (Bishop 61)	Pennock
Horlock	Southall
Brown (Vaughan 61)	Galloway (Saunders 56)
Whitley	Hessenthaler
Cooke	Smith
Dickov	Taylor
Goater	Asaba (Carr 87)

I N MAY 1999, arguably, Manchester City's renaissance really began. The Blues had endured a nervy, unimpressive first campaign in the nation's third tier and for long periods it seemed as though Joe Royle's side were destined to spend another season down among the dead men and who knows what implications that may have had on the club's future had that actually happened?

City were mid-table and heading nowhere by early December with the low point undoubtedly a 2-1 defeat away to York City underlining just how far this famous old club had fallen from grace.

But Royle's men dug deep and gradually began to turn things around and a sustained run of form in the race for the play-offs started around the turn of the year and the Blues sustained enough form to finish in the top six, pitting them against Wigan Athletic for the right to face the winners of the game between Preston North End and Gillingham at Wembley Stadium.

City drew the first leg against the Latics 1-1 at Springfield Park and won the second leg 1-0 courtesy of a Shaun Goater goal while Gillingham surprisingly saw off much-fancied Preston over two legs to set up a showdown in the capital. There was a real frenzy for tickets at both clubs, with the Blues asking for 50,000 and Gillingham 40,000 – the only trouble was that Wembley only held 80,000!

City argued their average crowd was 30,000 compared with Gillingham's 8,000 or so, but the FA deigned that the share should be equal, causing a great deal of anger and frustration that the tickets weren't handed out in a way that better reflected each team's true following – not just the fly-by-nights who fancied a day out at Wembley.

Ultimately, City were given around 40,000 and Gillingham only slightly less and a record crowd for a Second Division play-off was guaranteed.

The Blues were the bookies' favourites to triumph, particularly as they had appeared 11 times in various Wembley finals whereas this was the Gills' inaugural appearance at the Twin Towers.

City had injury concerns over skipper Andy Morrison and Ian Bishop but both men were named in the squad with Morrison starting and Bishop on the bench – the latter's exclusion from the starting line-up causing much chagrin among the Blues' followers who felt the classy midfielder could make the difference on Wembley's wide-open spaces. Only time would tell.

From early in the game it was clear that Gillingham were in the final on merit and that this was going to be a close match. Plus Gills keeper Vince Bartram – Paul Dickov's close friend – was in inspired form.

The longer the game went on, the more nervy the City fans became, fearing one goal might be enough to settle the game either way, though expecting the worst.

The limping Morrison was withdrawn and replaced by Tony Vaughan just past the hour and Michael Brown gave way to Bishop at the same time. Immediately City looked more cohesive as Bishop sprayed balls around the park in imperious fashion.

With extra time looking likely, disaster struck when Carl Asaba burst through the City defence to toe-poke the ball into the roof of the net for Gillingham on 81 minutes. The City players and supporters were crest-fallen and it was going to take a monumental effort to claw their way back into the game.

Paul Dickov saw a point-blank shot saved by Bartram as the Blues chased an equaliser, but spaces appeared at the back and five minutes later Asaba back-heeled Robert Taylor through on goal and the Gillingham striker made it 2-0.

'Bye, bye Division Two!' crowed commentator Alan Brazil. 'It's party time in Kent tonight!' Who could blame him?

By the time the teams kicked off, there were 87 minutes on the clock and it looked as though it was game, set and match to Tony Pulis's side, but two minutes later, with thousands of City fans on their way out of Wembley, Kevin Horlock pulled one back with a low drive but to many, it was little more than scant consolation.

Then the board for added time went up and referee Mark Halsey indicated for five extra minutes. Suddenly there was belief and enough time to save the game – or was there?

As the minutes ticked agonisingly by, the ball was launched upfield by Wiekens, and nodded on by third sub Gareth Taylor towards Goater.

Goater's shot was charged down and the ball fell to Dickov 15 yards out. With 95 minutes played, this was it, the last chance saloon – seconds later one end of Wembley went bananas as Dickov lashed the ball into the roof of the net.

Extra time brought close calls at either end, but it seemed a penalty shoot-out was going to be the only way to separate the two sides.

City went first through Horlock who drilled the ball home for 1-0. Nicky Weaver then saved Gillingham's first effort but hero Dickov saw his spot kick hit one post, then the other before rebounding out. Incredibly, Gillingham missed their next penalty, too, with Weaver not even required to make a save as the ball sailed past the post.

Terry Cooke tucked his effort past Bartram to make it 2-0 before the Gills finally found the back of the net.

Richard Edghill cracked his kick in off the underside of the bar meaning if Gillingham missed their fourth penalty, City were up – and they did, as Weaver made his second save of the shoot-out before setting off on a celebratory run that has become part of City folklore.

It doesn't matter that this game was a Second Division play-off final. It doesn't matter that the team the Blues beat was Gillingham and not Real Madrid – this was, quite simply, one of the most exciting games in the club's history and a day those who witnessed it will never forget.

v Burnley 2-0

22 December 1973
First Division
Attendance: 28,114

MANCHESTER CITY:	BURNLEY:
MacRae	Stevenson
Pardoe	Noble
Donachie	Newton
Doyle	Dobson
Booth	Waldron
Towers	Ingham
Summerbee	Nulty
Bell	Hankin
Marsh	Fletcher
Lee	Collins
Leman	James

A DISTINCTLY AVERAGE season threatened to get worse after an alarming autumnal dip in form by Ron Saunders' team saw the Blues slip from sixth place to 14th by mid-December.

Just three wins in 14 was and a worrying lack of goals was slightly improved by an impressive 2-0 win at Tottenham the week before third-placed Burnley were due at Maine Road.

Denis Law was unfit for the visit of the Clarets, but Franny Lee was back in after missing the Spurs match as City chased a sixth win in nine home games. The Blues had all the incentive they needed to beat Burnley having already lost 1-0 at Maine Road back in August in the FA Charity Shield. Worse still, City had also been beaten 3-0 at Turf Moor by Jimmy Adamson's newly-promoted side.

During that game, Joe Corrigan was at fault for a couple of goals and in later years, former skipper Mike Doyle would recall that the Blues had complete control of the game when things started to go wrong.

Said Doyle, 'We were murdering Burnley at Turf Moor but we hadn't scored. Then one of Colin Bell's mates, Colin Waldron of all people, hit a 40-yard ball that I was about to head clear but Joe shouted for me to leave it. I moved out of the way and glanced around in time to see it go through his legs and into the net.

'Later in the game Joe shouted at his sparring partner Tommy Booth to pass the ball back which he did. The ball somehow again went through his legs. He tried to reach through instead of turning around and a Burnley player slid in to just send the ball over the line.

'Joe had scrambled back, slid into the net and got his feet entangled in the netting and lay there, stranded on his back. Tommy turned to me and said, "Look at him. He looks like a fucking beached whale".'

Corrigan soon lost his place to Keith MacRae, a £200,000 signing from Motherwell, and he would have to re-invent himself both mentally and physically to eventually regain his place and become one of the club's greatest keepers in the process.

But that was in the future.

A mixture of heavy rain and a sustained spell of overcast Mancunian weather meant the Maine Road pitch had cut up quite badly by late December and a crowd of just over 28,000 shivered under leaden and darkening skies.

The Blues had reached the quarter-finals of the League Cup and came into the game having drawn 2-2 at Coventry City three days before so the promise of silverware kept the campaign ticking along, but the need to win the last match before Christmas was evident in the tense opening exchanges between the sides.

The Blues felt hard done to from their earlier tussles with the Clarets and were keen for a bit of payback.

Despite this, it was, if anything, Burnley's football that looked more coherent and dangerous with several neat passing moves threatening early on.

MacRae justified Saunders's faith as he made a brilliant save to keep the score 0-0 – it proved to be a pivotal stop, too, as it was the Blues who finally broke the deadlock thanks to some shoddy defending from the visitors.

The ball found its way out to Rodney Marsh on the left and the elegant forward seemed to have overrun the ball as the full-back approached. However, the hapless Claret stumbled and Marsh was able to take the ball back and cross to the back post where Colin Bell headed home.

Little else of note happened before the break and City came out for the second half looking for a killer second, but again, James and Dobson drove

Burnley forward in search of an equaliser only to be continually repelled by Mike Doyle and Tommy Booth.

Lee tried to dance down the wing before being fouled and moments later Dobson clattered him again resulting in Lee attempting to take matters in his own hands as he aimed a kick at the Burnley man, fortunately missing his quarry, though he was clearly wound up by what appeared to be a deliberate attempt to induce a reaction.

The best move of the game came when Willie Donachie won the ball on the left, played a one-two with Lee and then moved into the Clarets' half. As the young Scot fed Marsh, the main problem of the Blues' once rapier counter-attack became clear as Marsh trapped the ball, waiting several seconds before switching play to the other flank.

An exasperated Lee waved his arms in despair as the opportunity dissipated and the accusations that Marsh's style just didn't fit into this team garnered yet more weight.

City needed a second goal to settle the crowd down and midway through the second period, they got it.

Mike Summerbee had been having one of his quieter games, but it was his left-wing corner than was met full on by Doyle whose header thundered in off the crossbar to make it 2-0.

It was no more than Saunders's side deserved and but for an outrageous linesman's flag, the score would have been 3-0 after Lee ghosted in at the back post to toe-poke the ball past Stevenson late on – TV replays proved he was a good yard onside, but the goal was scrubbed off.

City's patchy season would see them finish in 14th – their lowest place since 1967 – as well as lose the League Cup Final 2-1 to Wolves at Wembley Stadium.

Saunders, who had proved an unpopular figure in the dressing room where his disciplinarian style rubbed one too many the wrong way, paid the ultimate price before the campaign ended when he was sacked while Burnley went on to finish a highly creditable fifth in the table.

v West Bromwich A 6-1

44

3 August 1968
Charity Shield
Attendance: 35,510

MANCHESTER CITY:	WEST BROMWICH ALBION:
Mulhearn	Osborne (Merrick)
Connor	Fraser
Pardoe	Williams
Doyle	Lovett
Heslop	Talbut
Oakes	Kaye
Lee	Stephens
Bell	Brown
Summerbee	Krzywicki
Owen	Collard
Young	Hartford

BACK IN the days when charity began at home – literally – reigning league champions City took on FA Cup holders West Bromwich Albion in the annual top-flight curtain raiser.

It was the Blues' fourth Charity Shield match having lost 4-0 against Arsenal in 1934, beaten Sunderland 2-0 in 1937 and lost 1-0 to Manchester United in 1956. Having won the title on the final day of the 1967/68 season, the Blues had embarked on a mammoth month-long tour of the USA and the exhausted squad managed just one win in nine games against teams they would have normally been expected to beat with ease.

The fatigue would follow them into the new season, but as in this game, there were moments when it was clear to see City were still a cut above the rest of the division when the mood took them.

The Charity Shield venue was generally the home ground of the league champions with Wembley not considered a deserving site for a match that was little more than a showpiece friendly.

Sprinkled among the City fans were Albion supporters and even a Liverpool flag was spotted on the Kippax – strange days indeed, but as charity began at home, there was no reported crowd trouble on the day.

With partially re-charged batteries, Joe Mercer's side, featuring new signing Bobby Owen, walked out to a sun-drenched Maine Road in front of a more than respectable 35,510 fans with something of a point to prove.

Albion had beaten City twice in five days on their way to the title and had been the only team to record a league double that season – an anomaly in an otherwise excellent campaign but one that very nearly cost City the title.

The home support was still in celebratory mood, fully expecting their team to challenge strongly for the title once again and with the prospect of a first foray into the European Cup to look forward to, it was a period of unprecedented optimism for the blue half of the city.

The BBC were in town covering the game for their *Match of the Day* highlights show later that evening and the great Ken 'they think it's all over' Wolstenholme provided the commentary. What nobody expected was West Brom to take the word charity to heart with a series of comical mistakes in their defence from start to finish.

With barely a minute on the clock, a youthful Asa Hartford played a poor pass into the middle that Colin Bell easily intercepted and then quickly played a 40-yard ball into the path of Mike Summerbee on the right flank.

Summerbee spotted Owen's intelligent run and played a superb cross into his path and the former Bury striker deftly placed the ball past Osborne in the Baggies' goal to get his City career off to a flying start – a goal inside 60 seconds with his first touch. It doesn't get much better than that.

Bell was dominating the middle of the park and he sprayed the ball out to Summerbee whose tempting cross was nodded into his own goal by Lovett to put City 2-0 up but it was the third goal that proved just how brilliant and influential Bell, Francis Lee and Summerbee were to this magnificent Mercer/Allison side.

A free kick on the edge of the box suggested Lee was shaping up to smash the ball goalwards – the crowd thought as much and the Albion defenders certainly were convinced, but Lee ran past the ball as Bell instead passed to Summerbee on the penalty spot. Summerbee then passed to Lee who had continued his run and the Blues' number 9 slotted the ball home to make it 3-0.

It was so simple, yet brilliant and innovative and it had the home crowd in raptures.

Albion pulled a goal back on the stroke of half-time through Krzywicki who broke through and rounded Ken Mulhearn with aplomb to reduce the arrears and give the travelling fans something to cheer, but their joy was short-lived.

Merrick replaced Osborne in goal at the break but the new Albion keeper's first job was to pick the ball out of the net after he allowed Owen's tame shot to somehow emerge from under his dive and trickle over the line.

Terrible defending not long after meant Mike Doyle's hopeful punt into the box suddenly became a good scoring chance for Neil Young after Fraser completely missed his attempt at a headed clearance and Young made no mistake with a rocket shot past the hapless Merrick who wasn't being helped by the Fred Karno-type circus defending in front of him.

The sixth and final goal was again partly down to goalkeeping that left much to be desired. Alan Oakes fed Bell on the left and his looping cross found Summerbee who nodded down to Lee.

Lee's shot was straight at Merrick who capped a woeful display as he crouched to collect the ball by allowing it to somehow evade his grasp and trickle home for number six.

For Albion, the final whistle couldn't come quickly enough on a day nobody from the Black Country will want to remember.

Incredibly, the Blues almost gave West Brom a repeat dose of medicine in the league meeting four months later, winning 5-1 in the league at Maine Road, but by then, an oddly out-of-sorts City had slipped to 16th in the table, some six wins and 13 points adrift of league leaders Liverpool.

Still, the Baggies had been made to pay in full for their impudence the season before.

v Newcastle United 4-3

11 May 1968
First Division
Attendance: 46,300

MANCHESTER CITY:	NEWCASTLE UNITED:
Mulhearn	McFaul
Book	Craig
Pardoe	Clark
Doyle	Moncur
Heslop	McNamee
Oakes	Iley
Lee	Sinclair
Bell	Scott
Summerbee	Davies
Young	B. Robson
Coleman	T. Robson

CITY HAVE had more than their fair share of last-day dramas and in May 1968, one of the club's biggest dates awaited. The entire 1967/68 season boiled down to one match for City who went into the final game away to Newcastle United in pole position in the First Division.

Manchester United were level on points with the Blues and were home to Sunderland – it was clearly the Blues who had the tougher task and this was reflected by the bookies making the Reds slight favourites to lift the title.

Newcastle at St James' Park was always a daunting proposition and the Magpies had a passionate and demanding home crowd to please no matter what the situation. With the chance of a first title for 31 years, an estimated 20,000 City fans made their way to the north-east to cheer on Joe Mercer's men who had been a Second Division side just two years before.

With no injury concerns before kick-off, the Blues fielded the side that had started the majority of games that campaign and the match got off to a lively start with the nerves clearly on show as neither side seemed capable of stringing more than two passes together.

As a result, chances were going begging at either end. It was rare the home fans were outshouted on their own patch but the roars of 'City! City!

City!' were soon echoing around the ground, though it was Newcastle who came within a whisker of opening the scoring as Scott rattled the bar with a 20-yard shot that had Ken Mulhearn well beaten.

However, the travelling hordes didn't have long to wait for the opening goal. Mike Summerbee won a free kick on the right and Doyle played a quick pass to Colin Bell. Bell took the ball towards the corner flag before finding Doyle on the edge of the box and he whipped in a cross that Summerbee fired into the roof of the net from close range to put City ahead.

Pockets of City fans began to celebrate all around St James' Park and if anyone had been in doubt as to how many Mancunians there were in the capacity crowd, they were instantly dismissed.

Boos rang out from the home fans and there were one or two scuffles but order was soon restored. Even more so, perhaps, within 60 seconds because Newcastle hauled themselves level after George Heslop's surge forward came to an abrupt end just past the halfway line.

It left the Blues short at the back and when a long clearance upfield followed, the ball landed at the feet of Sinclair who found himself a yard of space, dropped his shoulder and spotted the prolific Pop Robson in acres of space on the edge of the box. Robson touched the ball ahead and then finished with a powerful drive across Mulhearn to make it 1-1.

Wyn Davies continued to cause problems in the air and his looping header was headed off the line by skipper Tony Book as the hosts turned up the heat. Clearly the Blues were going to have to be at their best to win this game.

There were few more attractive sides than City on their day and the free-flowing football and attacking talent within the teams meant there would always be more chances and on the half-hour, the Blues went ahead again with Neil Young reacting first to Alan Oakes's deflected shot to make it 2-1 with a typically clinical finish from the edge of the box.

It was the mark of champions when a team could sustain so much pressure and then causally slip through the gears to re-take the lead.

But just as before, the Magpies hit back straight away and Jackie Sinclair made it 2-2 shortly after with a stunning 20-yard drive that sailed past Mulhearn into the top right-hand corner. It was turning out to be a nail-biting, thrilling affair.

The Blues raced out of the blocks after the break and Young was again on target shortly after the re-start as Bell lost two defenders with a smart turn on the edge of the box that caused confusion before Young stabbed home from close range.

Then Bell fed Franny Lee who dashed clear to deftly chip home the fourth just past the hour-mark as City finally established a two-goal cushion.

The celebrations began off the pitch but they certainly didn't on it where there was still plenty of work to do and with five minutes remaining the Blues' resolve cracked again as Newcastle centre-back John McNamee headed home a terrific Pop Robson cross to reduce the arrears and make it 4-3.

In a frantic finale, City tried to keep the ball and play down time but the Magpies refused to lay down and die – it was almost too much to bear for the watching City fans who had thought the game and the points had already been wrapped up.

Then, finally, referee Kirkpatrick had seen enough and blew for full time. The City fans poured on to the pitch to celebrate – the Blues were champions.

It didn't matter what United's result was, the Blues had deservedly won the title by playing a brand of football that was both stylish and swashbuckling and the victory at St James' Park had demonstrated as much.

For the record, the Reds went down 2-1 at Sunderland to end their campaign like a damp squib and Liverpool, hovering with a game in hand in third, finished as runners-up.

With an established side made up of players who were mostly in their early to mid-20s, many expected City to dominate English football and perhaps Europe for years to come but it would be another 44 years before they tasted title glory again.

46 v Aston Villa 5-1

23 April 1991
First Division

MANCHESTER CITY:	ASTON VILLA:
Coton	Spink
Hill	Price
Pointon	Gage
Hendry	McGarth
Harper	Comyn (Cascarino)
Redmond	Nielsen
Brennan	Daley
Ward	Platt
Heath	Olney
White	Cowans
Quinn	Penrice

THERE ARE some nights in football that have an electrically-charged crackle before a ball has even been kicked. City's trip to Villa Park came just ten days before the end of a solid season under player-manager Peter Reid and there was a chance of a top five finish for the first time in 13 years, not to mention the possibility of ending up higher than United – something that hadn't happened since 1978.

The evening midweek kick-off would have been the perfect excuse for vast empty spaces in the away end, but something caught the imagination of the City fans about this fixture and more than 5,000 made the trip down the M6, hell-bent on enjoying the match.

There was a party atmosphere among the travelling throngs who easily out-shouted the relegation-threatened hosts who were precariously placed just above the drop zone.

Despite the Villains' position, prior to the previous Saturday they had lost just one of their 16 home games that season but a nervy 2-1 defeat at the hands of Wimbledon had increased their winless run to six and left them on the brink of Second Division football.

City had won just four of their 17 away games going into the match so a bookmaker would probably have edged towards a score draw as the most likely outcome.

With the raucous backing of the visiting support, City began confidently, perhaps sensing the nervousness of the home players and David White went close after just a couple of minutes. Then, in the fifth minute, White struck the first goal of what would be a memorable night for himself and for the Blues.

A smart exchange of passes between Niall Quinn and Mark Brennan saw the latter play a clever ball into the path of White who buried a low shot past Nigel Spink to put the Blues ahead.

The goal sparked Villa into life and they were unlucky not to be awarded a spot kick as a smart cross-field pass appeared to be handled in the box by Brennan. Then Ian Olney was denied an equaliser by a brave stop from Tony Coton – the scourge of the home fans having played for Birmingham City but if Coton was to be cast as the pantomime villain, he was going to enjoy himself.

It was his mammoth clearance that was flicked on by Quinn and then lobbed home by White that increased the Blues' lead – playing in white shirts and blue shorts incidentally – to make it 2-0.

Then Coton saved brilliantly again from Olney as the Villa fans probably realised it wasn't going to be their night. David Platt's miss in a one-on-one situation with Coton just after that confirmed as much.

City went in at the break 2-0 to the good and started the second half where they had left off and were unlucky not to go three ahead when Neil Pointon's deep cross found Quinn who teed up Mark Ward on the edge of the box and the former West Ham star thumped a half-volley against the post, just missing out on what would have been a spectacular team goal.

No matter – soon after, City did go 3-0 up and it was the red-hot White again who was at the heart of the move that saw him race clear down the right before picking out Brennan with a low cross that the midfielder side-footed home.

Villa were handed an unlikely lifeline when Gary Penrice's persistence set up Platt from close range and Steve Redmond's clearance on the line was harshly adjudged to have been with his arm. TV replays proved otherwise but Platt converted the penalty to reduce the arrears to two goals.

But City, and White in particular, were far from finished. Any hopes Villa had of working their way back into the game were ended when Quinn's sliding tackle put White clear on goal and as Spink came out to narrow the angle the City forward side-footed a drive that fairly flew into the net off the post to send the away fans wild and guarantee three points.

The White and Quinn partnership had been one of the highlights of the season and the pair complemented each other perfectly. The towering Quinn needed the merest flick on knowing White's electric pace would win any contest for the ball and the rest was up to White's finishing.

On this night, he had been as good as any striker in Europe – practically unplayable – which was why so often he cut a frustrating figure because days like this were all too rare for a such a talented striker/winger.

There was still time for White to score his fourth goal of the game, cutting in from the right before striking a low drive that beat Spink on his near post to confirm an emphatic 5-1 victory for City. The Mancunian hordes lapped it up and headed home after a thoroughly enjoyable evening out.

There were still two games to play and though the enthusiasm was dampened somewhat a few days later with a 1-0 defeat at Old Trafford in the Manchester derby, City ended the season with a thrilling 3-2 victory over Sunderland to confirm fifth position in the table – one place higher than the Reds – and end a very satisfactory first full campaign under Reid's leadership.

As for Villa, they conceded five more goals a few days later as Leeds United beat them 5-2 at Elland Road, but a 2-1 home win over Norwich City and a 2-2 last-day draw with Chelsea saw them avoid relegation.

In fact, they had City to thank for their top-flight survival as it had been the Blues who had relegated Derby County and Sunderland in a season where only two clubs went down.

v Barnsley 7-1

21 September 2004
League Cup second round
Attendance: 19,578

MANCHESTER CITY:	BARNSLEY:
Waterreus	Colgan
Thatcher (Jordan 48)	Hassell
Distin (Sommeil 45)	T. Williams
Mills	Kay
Jihai	R. Williams (Boulding 31)
Flood	Shuker (Nardiello 66)
Barton	Wroe
Bosvelt	McPhail
Sibierski	Burns
S. Wright-Phillips	Conlon
Macken (B. Wright-Phillips 46)	Chopra

BARNSLEY ARRIVED at what was then still the City of Manchester Stadium for the second round of the Carling Cup knowing they faced an uphill task to progress in the competition.

Kevin Keegan picked a strong side for the tie and the Tykes brought more than 5,000 fans across the Pennines to swell a disappointing crowd to just fewer than 20,000.

The Blues had made an average start to the 2004/05 campaign, taking seven points from a possible 18, though six of them had come in the previous three games with wins over Charlton Athletic and Crystal Palace suggesting better times lay ahead.

The Carling Cup offered a welcome distraction for the players and an opportunity to record a morale-boosting win over the Tykes with a seemingly difficult campaign ahead – but even the most optimistic City fans couldn't have expected the goal-feast that was to follow.

Barnsley began brightly, perhaps realising that they had to grasp the opportunity and try and rattle their hosts rather than defend deep and hope to nick extra time then a penalty shoot-out.

In fact, they were more than holding their own in the opening exchanges and with 20 minutes gone, the score was still 0-0 and frustration among the home fans was starting to grow – but that opening spell was as good as it got as City then banged five goals past Tykes keeper Nick Colgan in the space of 24 frantic minutes to render the tie well and truly over by the break.

Joey Barton started the rout on 21 minutes with a cracking effort from distance and immediately the visitors' heads dropped. With Shaun Wright-Phillips arguably at the peak of his game and causing mayhem in Barnsley's defence, Jon Macken made it 2-0 on 28 minutes and Academy graduate Willo Flood added a third in – aptly – the 33rd minute to make it 3-0.

Barnsley's defence looked shell-shocked and there was worse to some as Wright-Phillips sent a delightful chip over Colgan to make it 4-0 on 36 minutes with City continuing to run wild.

There was more to come, too, as Macken doubled his tally a minute before the break to make it 5-0 before the teams traipsed off for their half-time refreshments.

It had been a blistering spell by Keegan's side who proved that when they were firing on all cylinders, they were a match for anyone.

Memories of the ten-goal haul against another South Yorkshire side came flooding back with those who witnessed the 10-1 win over Huddersfield in 1987 wondering if they might be about to see another historic evening. And why not?

Barnsley had only their pride to play for and unless they were given the right pep talk in the dressing room, they would surely continue their capitulation, but as it was, they started the second half in the best manner possible with a goal within 90 seconds of the re-start and the scorer – former City player Barry Conlon – enjoyed the moment and earned a generous (if not slightly patronising) reception from the home fans.

Conlon represented an era not so long ago when the Blues were forced to buy lower league bargains and journeyman players.

The visiting fans chanted ironically that they were on for a 6-5 victory but within ten minutes, City's five-goal cushion had been restored with Antoine Sibierski giving the irrepressible Wright-Phillips his third assist of the night to make it 6-1.

Managed by boyhood City supporter Paul Hart – the son of former City player and manager Johnny Hart – Barnsley put up a better show as Kevin Keegan's side took their foot off the gas, but Sibierski added a seventh six minutes from time to rub salt in the Tykes' wounds and complete the rout and make it 7-1 on the night. For Keegan it was a flash of the sort of football he had wanted City to play, but had become all-too rare of late.

For the 15,000 or so home fans who came out on a crisp early autumn evening, the trip had been well worthwhile. For the travelling thousands preparing to travel back over the Woodhead Pass, they at least headed home knowing they had accepted the defeat in good heart, painful though it had been and that for at least two 20-minute spells during the game, their players had given it a good go.

The Blues hadn't managed ten goals but they had set a new stadium record biggest win, which was something and it wasn't every day seven goals were scored by one team in a game.

City, hoping to end the long wait for silverware, needed a decent draw to progress further in the competition that had last brought glory in 1976, and pulled reigning Premier League champions Arsenal – the side who had been dubbed 'The Invincibles' after going the entire 2003/04 campaign unbeaten in the league – out of the hat for the third round.

Not only were the Gunners the best side in the country, they were also a team the Blues had hardly beaten at all home or away for the best part of three decades – and City duly exited stage left to Arsene Wenger's men, losing 2-1 at home.

As for Keegan, the emotional boss quit his role as the Blues' chief later that season, claiming he could no longer motivate the squad he had assembled. Stuart Pearce took the position on, initially in a caretaker capacity, but the seven-goal feat against the Tykes remained one of the season's highlights.

v Sheffield Wednesday 6-2

48

22 September 2001
First Division
Attendance: 25,731

MANCHESTER CITY:	SHEFFIELD WEDNESDAY:
Weaver	Pressman
Edghill (Dunne 45)	McLaren (Lescott 64)
Howey	Westwood
Wiekens	Maddix
Pearce	Bromby
Etuhu	Quinn
Benarbia (Horlock 80)	Soltvedt
Tiatto	Palmer
Granville	Morrison (Hamshaw 80)
Goater (Huckerby 74)	Bonvin (Donnelly 86)
Wanchope	Di Piedi

THE 2001/02 season had begun in typical Kevin Keegan style with plenty of goals at either end and a mixture of brilliance in attack and kamikaze defending that were a trademark of the new City boss throughout his managerial career.

His ethos of 'we'll score more goals than you' had been apparent in the first seven games of which the Blues had won four and lost three.

It was hard to fathom which City would turn up on the day at Hillsborough but with a total of 32 goals in the matches involving the Blues up to that point, it seemed certain there would be plenty of entertainment.

City were looking to improve on the away form that had seen one win and three losses with Norwich, Coventry and West Brom all triumphing on their own patch fairly comfortably.

Sheffield Wednesday were still awaiting their first home win so, on paper, this looked like a good chance for Keegan's side to show the kind of form that had brought them maximum points from their three First Division home games to date.

Ali Benarbia had joined a week before on a free transfer and had made an instant impact on his debut against Birmingham and was afforded a standing ovation by the Maine Road crowd. The Algerian playmaker was magical on the ball with the vision of a world-class midfielder that made him an instant favourite. He had found the net in midweek during a 4-3 defeat by Coventry City and would have his best game yet against the Owls.

Wednesday were injury hit and had several youngsters drafted into the senior team, but that shouldn't detract one iota from the performance City were about to give, though it began with the kind of haphazard defending that was stopping Keegan's men climbing to the summit – the Blues currently occupied a somewhat underwhelming eighth and could drop into mid-table unless they left the Steel City with three points.

Backed by around 6,000 travelling fans, City were behind within two minutes when Pablo Bonvin bundled home a cross from the right that should have been cleared and it was a lead the Owls held until past the half-hour mark. The Blues' football had been fluid and threatening but the young Wednesday side had held firm.

Then, on 32 minutes, the breakthrough came as Stuart Pearce's corner was cleared to the left-hand side of the Sheffield box when Benarbia picked up, dropped his shoulder one way then went the other before firing a low drive in that beat Kevin Pressman on his near post to level the scores.

Three minutes later, City were ahead as Pearce's long ball found Shaun Goater who stole stole in between Ashley Westwood and Pressman before deftly lobbing the keeper from a tight angle to make it 2-1.

It was his tenth of the campaign already and just before the break he almost made it 3-1, arriving on the back post as Danny Tiatto's cross came in but he slid the ball inches wide. It was a tad harsh on the Owls who were down, but certainly not out of the game and – just as they had in the first half – within moments of the second half beginning, the home fans were celebrating again as defender Leigh Bromby equalised with a powerful header from a set-piece that gave boyhood Wednesday fan Nicky Weaver no chance.

In fact, Bromby had been linked with City throughout the summer and he showed why when he carried the ball from the halfway line to the edge of the box only to see his low shot parried away by Weaver.

The home fans tried to roar their team on, sniffing an unlikely win but the pendulum soon swung back in City's favour as Benarbia picked out wing-back Danny Granville on the edge of the Wednesday box who chested it to Goater who returned the perfect pass for Granville to go on and finish from close range.

This time there was to be no way back for the hosts as the Blues shifted up a couple of gears with the brilliant Benarbia at the heart of everything. As Richard Dunne's long throw was cleared by the Owls' defence, Benarbia was again waiting and his weighted chip across was inch perfect for Paulo Wanchope to get the merest of flicks that sent the ball away from Pressman's reach and into the net for the fourth of the afternoon for City – all in front of the vast travelling army who were lapping it all up and with only 68 minutes gone, there was time for more punishment.

Two minutes later, Benarbia spotted Tiatto's burst forward and played him in. The Australian defender held the ball up before giving it back to Benarbia who saw Goater's dart forward in the box and played a sumptuous ball into his path – the Bermudian deftly rounded Pressman before scoring from a tight angle to make it 5-2. This was attacking football of the highest calibre, but it wasn't quite over.

You had to feel a modicum of sympathy for Wednesday who were without the injured Gerald Sibon, Efan Ekoku and Tommy Johnson. Toothless in attack, over-run in midfield and increasingly absent at the back, they faced another 20 minutes against a rampant City side who were thirsty for more.

The Blues declared at six when Darren Huckerby was fouled in the box and Wanchope slammed home the spot kick to confirm a fantastic afternoon's football for the travelling hordes.

And what of the Algerian genius Benarbia? Wanchope summed him up perfectly when he said of his vision, 'He can see you when you can't even see yourself.'

Keegan added, 'The main plus for me was that the fans go home thinking, "We're going to enjoy watching this team". We keep shooting ourselves in the foot and we're not going to get away with it every day.'

That season, however, more often than not, Keegan's entertainers did get away with it as they went on to win the title with style, panache and plenty of goals.

49 v Manchester United 6-1

23 October 2011
Premier League
Attendance: 75,487

MANCHESTER CITY:	MANCHESTER UNITED:
Hart	De Gea
Richards	Smalling
Kompany	Ferdinand
Lescott	Evans
Clichy	Evra
Yaya Toure	Nani (Hernandez 65)
Barry	Fletcher
Milner (Kolarov 89)	Anderson (Jones 66)
Silva	Young
Balotelli (Dzeko 70)	Rooney
Aguero	Welbeck

CHANCES ARE if you could bundle up wishes and make them into reality, the events of 23 October 2011 would come close to realising every City fans' wildest dreams. To win at Old Trafford was rare enough, but to crush United in their own backyard was unheard of in modern times, especially for the Blues who had recorded just one win there in 37 painful years.

Sven-Goran Eriksson had presided over the ending of the hoodoo in 2008 when City won 2-1 to lay the ghost of Denis Law's back-heeled winner back in 1974 once and for all.

The Reds had managed to win the next three meetings on their own patch, including a Carling Cup semi-final second-leg victory and a last-gasp clincher in a 4-3 victory in the league.

So much was riding on this particular game, however, with City showing signs that they could also end another dearth in their record books – a first league title for 44 years. If Roberto Mancini's side were serious about taking United's crown, they would have to come away with something. A draw would be more than acceptable, but a win – now that really would put down a marker.

This was to be one of the most remarkable derbies of all time for a number of reasons, even by Manchester standards, and it ended with

City celebrating one of the biggest wins in the fixture's history and the humiliated ten-man Reds would be left nursing their wounded pride.

United had never conceded so many at home in the league and for many, it represented a watershed moment not only in Manchester football but the Premier League as well. Things would never be the same again and the confirmation that a new power in English football had arrived was confirmed during 90 unforgettable minutes.

With United unbeaten at home for 18 months, City would have to continue the form that had seen them take 22 from a possible 24 points after beginning the campaign at a blistering pace. Yet despite this, United were just two points adrift having kept on the Blues' shoulders from the word go.

United edged the opening exchanges but never really threatened Joe Hart so when James Milner pulled the ball back to the edge of the box Mario Balotelli arrived on cue send an exquisite low shot past David de Gea to give City a lead.

After being in the headlines for all the wrong reasons yet again following a house fire caused by fireworks, Balotelli celebrated by lifting his jersey to reveal a T-shirt emblazoned with the question 'Why Always Me?' – earning him an inevitable yellow card from referee Mark Clattenburg but he didn't care and the Blues held comfortably until the break.

Shortly after half-time, things were about to get a whole lot better for the Blues and again, Balotelli was heavily involved as Sergio Aguero played in the Italian who was clearly tugged back by United defender Jonny Evans and the referee had no option but to send him off.

A goal up and United down to ten men – a great scenario but there wasn't a City fan watching who thought it would be enough so when Silva, Milner and Balotelli combined to put the Blues 2-0 up, the celebrations among the 3,000 travelling fans were feverish. Milner burst into the United box before delivering a pinpoint cross for Balotelli to prod home at the far post.

A goal for the Reds would have tested City's mettle, but the visitors were by now in total command and on 70 minutes that authority was underlined as Balotelli's back-heel found Milner who in turn found the marauding Micah Richards who crossed to the back post where Aguero slid the ball home to put the Blues 3-0 up.

Darren Fletcher pulled one back for United after 80 minutes with a spectacular strike from the edge of the box to give Hart no chance, but City were far from finished and as the game ticked towards past the 90-minute mark, the Blues showed a ruthless streak by mercilessly punishing the Reds in injury time.

First substitute Edin Dzeko bundled in a fourth goal with his knee after Joleon Lescott pulled the ball back for him with Gareth Barry's header from a corner going wide.

City had scored four goals away to United – unheard of but, perhaps sensing the opportunity to write their names into the history books and be remembered for all time, the Blues clicked up another gear with some devastating football in the dying seconds.

Dzeko, having a stunning impact, drove into the United half before feeding Silva who took the ball into the box and then slipped it through the legs of de Gea for number five. City fans were in heaven and thought of the famous 5-1 win back in 1989 – but there was still one more twist of the knife to come.

With Old Trafford emptying at the rate of a fire drill, Silva took a difficult pass with consummate ease and in one movement, half-volleyed a sumptuous through ball for Dzeko to chase.

The Bosnian couldn't have asked for a better pass and he took it in his stride before finishing with a powerful low drive that de Gea could only get his fingertips to as the ball sped past him into the net.

Dzeko ran to the corner to celebrate with the City fans and the demolition derby was complete. A 6-1 win, a ten-goal goal difference swing and three points that gave the Blues a five-point lead. Who could have thought it was possible to have so much fun at Old Trafford?

v Stoke City 1-0

14 May 2011
FA Cup Final, Wembley Stadium
Attendance: 88,643

MANCHESTER CITY:	STOKE CITY:
Hart	Sorensen
Richards	Wilson
Kompany	Huth
Lescott	Shawcross
Kolarov	Wilkinson
De Jong	Pennant
Barry (Johnson 73)	Whelan (Pugh 84)
Yaya Toure	Delap (Carew 80)
Silva (Vieira 90)	Etherington (Whitehead 62)
Tevez (Zabaleta 87)	Walters
Balotelli	Jones

FOR A club that had waited 35 years to taste success again, this was an emotional afternoon for a generation of City fans who had grown up without seeing their team win a single trophy.

There had been a near miss in 1981 when the Blues twice led in the FA Cup Final against Spurs in the initial game and then the replay five days later, but apart from a League Cup semi-final and a play-off final victory, there had been nothing.

Roberto Mancini knew the club had to get the monkey off their back and bring a trophy home so the FA Cup had become the main focus of a side still a little short of seriously challenging for the title and more than hopeful of clinching a Champions League place.

The latter was still to be decided as cup final weekend was not the last fixture on the domestic calendar due to the Champions League Final taking place at Wembley a fortnight later.

City had breezed their way to the semi-final where Yaya Toure's second-half winner was enough to beat Manchester United 1-0 and they would start as red-hot favourites to win against Tony Pulis's Stoke.

The Potters had thrashed Bolton 5-1 in the other semi and were in the final on merit, but while their fans felt their name must be on the trophy, the City fans felt certain this was their time.

The West End of Wembley was a mass of sky blue with the 'Poznan' largely reserved for the pre-match announcement of the Stoke starting XI. It wasn't quite as impressive as the semi win over United and there were maybe 10,000 less City fans due to the ticket allocation for the 'football family', but it was effective nonetheless.

With the sun beating down on Wembley, the stage was set for what would hopefully be a classic game of football with, City fans hoped, a favourable outcome.

A crescendo of noise greeted the players with both sets of fans in fine voice and the critics who said the FA Cup had lost its lustre couldn't have failed to be impressed by what was a good old fashioned cup final contested between two who the game meant so much to.

Another couple of years of Manchester United v Chelsea or similar could well have sounded the death knell for the oldest domestic cup competition in the world.

For the superstitious among the 25,000 or so City fans – that's pretty much all 25,000 – to have the same end against Stoke as they'd had against United, plus Blues attacking the sea of blue after the break once again, was crucial. And the similarities wouldn't end there.

Skipper Carlos Tevez was recalled to the starting line-up after injury and Mancini also gave a starting berth to the erratic but occasionally brilliant Mario Balotelli. Aleks Kolarov also won selection ahead of Pablo Zabaleta.

Matthew Etherington and Robert Huth, Stoke's major pre-match doubts, both started for the Potters, but there was no great shock there.

The Blues made a fabulous start and the first 15 minutes were played almost exclusively in Stoke territory. Thomas Sorensen made a wonderful save from a Tevez drive and Yaya Toure shaved the post with a howitzer from outside the box.

The movement from Mancini's men was terrific, particularly from Balotelli who showed commendable discipline both in attack and defence as Stoke were forced into containment mode and were reliant on winning throw-ins on the halfway line to ease the pressure.

Sorensen's performance continued to get better as he brilliantly flew to claw away a curling Balotelli effort that was destined for the top corner and the more negative-thinking City fans wondered if their day of glory would be denied by a keeper having a 'worldy' – let's face it, we've all seen games like that before.

In fact, the Blues had chance after chance – none better than when Silva managed to miss from eight yards by driving his shot into the ground and over the bar when it looked easier to score.

Stoke were reduced to a parody of themselves by pumping long balls up front for Kenwyne Jones to contest as they sought to ease the almost continual pressure.

But for Sorensen, City would have been out of sight by the break as Stoke fell as flat as a day-old glass of Coke, perhaps overawed by the occasion – or more likely completely outplayed by a far superior side.

Still, the longer the game went on with the score 0-0, the more nervous the Blues' fans became – with justification. Jones had the first real clear-cut opening of the second half but his headlong charge was halted by the bravery of Joe Hart.

If City needed a reminder that the game was still on a knife-edge, that was surely it and it seemed to sharpen the Blues' focus at exactly the right time. Then on 74 minutes, came the moment all City fans had hoped would come but perhaps feared wouldn't as first Silva and then Balotelli had shots blocked only for Yaya Toure to hammer home the loose ball.

One end of Wembley went ballistic because there was surely no way back for Stoke who had been painfully average at best.

As Yaya was mobbed by his team-mates, there was a feeling of certainty that our moment had finally come and the Potters' limp response was that of a team physically and mentally spent.

The explosion of emotion on the full-time whistle was one of joy, relief and the realisation that, at last, the Blues were back and bringing a trophy home. A moment to cherish for thousands who believed the day may never come.

v Norwich City 6-1

14 April 2012
Premier League
Attendance: 26,812

MANCHESTER CITY:	NORWICH CITY:
Hart	Ruddy
Zabaleta	Martin
Kompany	R. Bennett
Lescott	Ward
Clichy	Drury
Silva (A. Johnson 76)	E. Bennett
De Jong	Howson
Barry	B. Johnson (Hoolahan 45)
Nasri (Yaya Toure 63)	Pilkington (Surman 45)
Aguero	Holt
Tevez (Richards 80)	Wilbraham (Morison 68)

CITY HAD nothing to lose. A defeat to Arsenal had left Roberto Mancini's men eight points adrift of leaders Manchester United with just six games remaining. A minor miracle was needed to give the Blues a chance of coming first in a title race which looked as good as over, but the players refused to give up on the dream that had seemed so tangible for the majority of the campaign.

The least City could do was end the season on a high and with a home derby against the Reds to come, there was a possibility that the gap could be just five points going into the final two games – it was something to cling to, even though there was no way on earth that Sir Alex Ferguson's side could possibly blow such an advantage.

Or so we thought. On the evening City thrashed West Brom 4-0, Wigan recorded a shock 1-0 win over United to reduce the gap to just five points – it was game on again, though United still had to drop a further five points.

City travelled to Norwich in good heart – they were going to end the campaign on a high even if it meant finishing runners-up so a game at one of the Blues' luckiest grounds represented the perfect opportunity to increase the pressure on United.

As the sun beat down on a packed Carrow Road, the Blues ran out with a spring in their step though it was the hosts who had the better of the opening exchanges and with their Premier League safety virtually assured after an impressive 3-2 win at Spurs, their verve and vigour was understandable.

But a moment of brilliance soon came from Carlos Tevez, only recently restored to the starting line-up after his one-man strike and three-month sojourn to Argentina.

The City striker collected the ball on the right and headed for goal before unleashing a vicious swerving shot that completely fooled John Ruddy in goal with 18 minutes on the clock.

Nine minutes later the lead was doubled and if the first goal had been impressive, the second was simply brilliant as Tevez received the ball on the edge of the box and laid off a back-heel for compatriot Sergio Aguero who thundered a spectacular shot past Ruddy to make it 2-0, a lead the Blues would hold until half-time.

Norwich, who had won seven of their previous eight home games, had to start the second period much better than they had ended the first, and they did as Andrew Surman lashed home a shot after Gareth Barry blocked Aaron Wilbraham's effort just six minutes after the re-start.

For a time it looked as if Paul Lambert's men might make a fist of it, but the Blues were far from finished and when Yaya Toure's shot was parried out by Ruddy and Tevez was on hand to make it 3-1 with 73 minutes on the clock rather take their foot off the gas, the onslaught continued. The Blues had already hit six on the road previously during the campaign with a 6-1 win over United at Old Trafford.

With Tevez in red-hot form, Aguero proved anything his compatriot could do, he could at least equal and his burst into the box and superb shot into the top-right corner to make it 4-1 just two minutes later was enough to seal the points for the visitors.

Tevez, however, was far from finished and he latched on to a weak back-pass on 80 minutes to calmly round Ruddy before rolling home his hat-trick and City's fifth. His redemption complete, he raced towards the stand housing the 2,500 or so City fans before stopping to take an imaginary golf swing – a dig at the press suggestions he had spent more time on the links than the pitch in the past few months.

It was typical Tevez – never a dull moment – and the City fans lapped it up. Not only that, their team were 5-1 up – the same score the meeting between the clubs at the Etihad Stadium had produced earlier in the campaign. His work for the afternoon complete, Tevez was then substituted as the Blues looked to inflict more hurt on their genial hosts.

Chances came and went but the Blues deservedly made it 6-1 on 90 minutes when a superb move saw Adam Johnson fire home from close range to complete the rout.

The win gave the Blues renewed home and momentum and though their task was still a tall order, it was the perfect boost at just the right time.

Canaries boss Paul Lambert said of his side's defeat, 'I think for 70-odd minutes we were well in the game. At 2-1 we looked really good and in the second half we played really well but if you're losing four goals in that space of time it was poor from our point of view. The effort was there in abundance, as it always is, but maybe the scoreline was severe.

'You can't legislate for losing three goals in seven minutes, and we'll learn from it. You take your medicine and you bounce back. Their strike force is incredible; the first two goals were world class. Our team have done brilliant, I can't be too harsh on them.'

A week later the Blues went to Wolves and won 2-0 and with the news Manchester United had blown a 4-2 lead over Everton to draw 4-4, it meant a win in the derby would put City top with two games to go. The rest, as they say, is history.

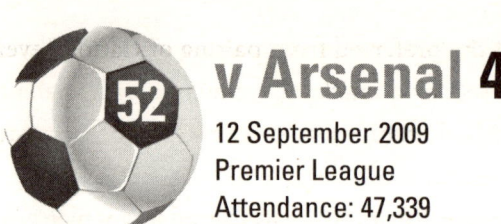

v Arsenal 4-2

12 September 2009
Premier League
Attendance: 47,339

MANCHESTER CITY:	ARSENAL:
Given	Almunia
Richards	Sagna (Eboue 77)
Kolo Toure	Gallas
Lescott	Vermaelen
Bridge	Clichy
De Jong	Song (Eduardo 77)
Wright-Phillips	Denilson (Rosicky 72)
Ireland (Petrov 73)	Bendtner
Barry	Fabregas
Bellamy	Diaby
Adebayor	Van Persie

WITH THREE Premier League wins out of three, Mark Hughes's City had started the season with a definite swagger that suggested exciting times were coming again.

A 2-1 win at Blackburn had been followed by a narrow 1-0 success over Wolves, a Carling Cup triumph at Crystal Place and another victory on the road, this time at Portsmouth.

Backed by new owner Sheikh Mansour's millions, Hughes's first season in charge hadn't quite gone as well as expected given the money spent, but the former Wales boss had made some solid signings nonetheless, bringing Shaun Wright-Phillips back to the club that made him a star and adding the likes of Nigel de Jong, Kolo Toure, Wayne Bridge, Robinho, Emmanuel Adebayor and Craig Bellamy over the course of his first 12 months in charge.

The pressure was on Hughes to deliver quickly and he continued to splash the cash for the 2009/10 campaign, bringing Gareth Barry and Joleon Lescott to the club – the latter, from Everton, was making his debut in this game as the Blues sought to prove they were worthy of a top four spot.

A win over Arsenal was rare enough, but three points and defeats for Chelsea and Manchester United could even see City top the division by the end of the day.

Though City were without the preferred front pairing of Carlos Tevez and Robinho, the scene was set for a cracking game and with the sun beating down on a packed Etihad Stadium, two teams looking to score goals and entertain began the match.

Adebayor's acrimonious departure from Arsenal ensured he got plenty of stick from the 3,000 travelling fans who began singing derisory songs about the Togo striker almost from the word go. Few imagined the fireworks that were to follow in this most explosive encounter.

Both teams started brightly but the Gunners were the more impressive as they stroked the ball around confidently at what had previously been a happy hunting ground. Despite this, it was City who edged ahead after 20 minutes when Micah Richards's towering header looped over Manuel Almunia, struck the inside of the post and went in off the keeper to send the pumped-up home fans wild.

The Adebayor factor was giving the occasion extra spice and it seemed there was little love lost between him and his former team-mates but on 62 minutes it was they who were celebrating as Robin van Persie's low drive beat Shay Given to make it 1-1. At that point, it seemed there would be only one winner as the north Londoners stepped up the ante.

But the Blues resisted and on 74 minutes the excellent Craig Bellamy was rewarded when his powerful shot beat Almunia to make it 2-1. It was the start of a fantastic ten-minute spell for Hughes's side who picked the Gunners apart with some swashbuckling attacking play and on 80 minutes City went 3-1 up – it just had to be the man of the moment Adebayor.

Wright-Phillips skipped down the right before delivering the perfect cross for Adebayor to head home from close range. His celebration, fuelled by adrenaline and pure anger, saw him sprint 80 yards from one end of the pitch to the other to finish with a knee-slide in front of the travelling fans and very nearly cause a riot.

It was foolish, of course, but there wasn't a City fan inside the ground who didn't enjoy the moment. It was also his fourth goal in his first four games – a blistering start to his career in sky blue that sadly probably peaked in this game.

And four minutes after that, Wright-Phillips raced through to deftly chip Almunia and make it 4-1 to almost blow the roof as the City fans went crazy. With just over five minutes remaining, the Blues just had to play out time for what was a stunning victory over a genuine title contender, but the drama wasn't quite over.

Thomas Rosicky pulled one back on 88 minutes and for the final two minutes plus maybe five minutes of injury time, the Gunners were superb, dominating totally and it's no exaggeration that they could have easily ended up taking a point home.

As it was, the Blues just about held firm to win 4-2 and maintain their 100 per cent record and were third in the table behind Chelsea and United (though with a game in hand).

Had Hughes fashioned a side worthy of a title challenge? Surely this win was a statement of intent and the derby at Old Trafford a week later would really test the Blues' mettle. Well, it did, and though City would slug it out blow for blow with the Reds, a last-gasp 4-3 win for United was the start of a downturn in fortunes for Hughes's team and he would lose his job to Roberto Mancini a few months later.

As for Adebayor, he was widely condemned for his celebration and was retrospectively handed a three-match ban for allegedly kicking van Persie in the face during the game.

Hughes later claimed Adebayor was emotional. 'We are delighted to come out on top against a very good Arsenal side,' he said. 'This was a challenge, which we passed. But there will be more.'

There was a feeling that Hughes came tantalisingly close to finding the right blend at City but perhaps didn't get the rub of the green at the right times. Either way, he progressed the team, made some excellent signings and should look back on his time with the Blues with some satisfaction.

v Burnley 6-1

3 April 2010
Premier League
Attendance: 21,330

MANCHESTER CITY:	BURNLEY:
Given	Jensen
Onuoha	Alexander
Sylvinho (De Jong 67)	Duff
Kolo Toure	Mears
Kompany	Cort
Johnson	Fox
Barry	McDonald (Cork 46)
Vieira	Eagles
Adebayor (Santa Cruz 79)	Fletcher (Paterson 80)
Tevez (Nimely 83)	Blake (Elliott 46)
Bellamy	Nugent

PLAYING AT Turf Moor always seems to bring out the best in City. It had been 36 years since the Blues had last lost to the Clarets in their own backyard and with five wins on the bounce in this fixture, Champions League-chasing City made the short journey north fully expecting to continue that sequence.

Facing a Saturday evening kick-off, Roberto Mancini's side were hoping to strengthen their challenge for fourth spot and improve their goal difference at the same time. Three points would see City leapfrog Spurs, who had surprisingly lost at Sunderland, as the race for the finish line ratcheted up a couple of notches.

It seemed only the torrential rain which had put the game in doubt could save Brian Laws's struggling side. The hosts had lost 12 of their previous 14 games and were spiralling out of the top flight at a rate of knots.

Shaun Goater used to call Burnley his 'ker-ching' club because he always filled his boots whenever he played them and though there would be no Goater for this game, City still cashed in with a breathless start.

The Blues were ahead with their first attack as Adam Johnson's corner found its way to Emmanuel Adebayor in the box. The Togo striker controlled the ball and then volleyed a powerful shot past Brian Jensen to give Mancini's side the perfect start.

There were just 66 seconds on the clock and three minutes later, City had doubled their advantage as Carlos Tevez played a pass towards Adebayor in the box but Craig Bellamy nipped in, wrong-footed the home defence and coolly slotted home from eight yards. Five minutes gone and 2-0 up, the Blues made it three just two minutes later when Jensen parried a low shot from Adebayor into the path of Tevez who tapped home from close range.

As late-comers took their seats, they were told that with seven minutes gone, the score was an improbable Burnley 0 Manchester City 3 – the question was how many were the Blues going to get with the Clarets already in turmoil?

Burnley were awful and the opening exchanges were more like a training match. The rain continued to fall and was gathering in places on the pitch but at least there were no more goals conceded by Burnley for the next 13 minutes – that meagre resistance ended in the 20th minute when Patrick Vieira headed home Johnson's corner to make it 4-0 to the visitors who showed no sign of easing up.

Burnley did stir for a spell, but it was too little and way too late. Many had already headed for the exits, disgusted at their team's efforts and while a goal might have made the game reasonably interesting for those who had bothered to stay, it was in fact City who scored the next goal with Tevez's superb through ball setting Adebayor clear to finish with a crisp low drive past Jensen.

It had been an incredible first half, but the main concern was now the incessant rain which continued to fall and as the teams traipsed off for the break, large puddles were now all over the pitch.

The home groundstaff were hardly going to jump through hoops to ensure the humiliation of their employers continued and though there was plenty of forking during the interval, there was still a strong possibility the match would not reach its conclusion.

Any serious injuries or blatantly weather-caused incidents would surely cause referee Alan Wiley to call a halt to proceedings. It had turned into a race against time.

City increased their lead just before the hour-mark with a third goal from a Johnson corner, this time Vincent Kompany's bullet header giving the hapless Jensen no chance.

There was still more than half an hour to go but the rain, if anything, was getting heavier. The game continued as some of the older travelling Blues in the 4,000 contingent present recalled a time when City were leading 6-2 at Luton – all the goals scored by Denis Law – only for the match to be abandoned with around 20 minutes left.

The conditions reduced the match to a lottery and the Blues' slick passing game was severely inhibited but the clock continued to tick towards full time and on 71 minutes Steven Fletcher pulled one back with a terrific finish as he burst free into the box and powered a shot past Shay Given.

That was as good as it got and there was relief when the referee finally blew for full time. It must have been a close call but there was no great outcry afterwards that the match should have been stopped.

Laws admitted his team had performed as badly as he had seen during his tenure, saying, 'The first six minutes was extraordinary and embarrassing. It's not acceptable. If you give them time and space like that, Manchester City are going to hurt you – and they took maximum advantage.

'I gave them a right roasting at half-time, and laid down an objective to the players not to lose the second half. At least they did that. But the first six minutes killed it all, and all we can do is apologise and respond before we play Hull.'

Mancini, meanwhile, was understandably satisfied, adding, 'I am very happy because we played a good game. The weather was not good, and in the second half it was difficult to play football.

'But we have six difficult games, and we must continue to improve in every game.'

As for City's hopes of ending in fourth, the run-in proved too problematical with the final nail in the coffin a galling 1-0 home defeat to Spurs which handed the north Londoners the place they had coveted.

v Tottenham Hotspur 5-1

54

28 August 2011
Premier League
Attendance: 36,150

MANCHESTER CITY:	TOTTENHAM HOTSPUR:
Hart	Friedel
Zabaleta (Richards 64)	Corluka
Kompany	Dawson
Lescott	Kaboul
Clichy	Assou-Ekotto
Yaya Toure	Lennon (Defoe 53)
Barry	Modric (Livermore 66)
Silva	Kranjcar (Huddlestone 46)
Nasri	Bale
Aguero (Savic 75)	Van der Vaart
Dzeko	Crouch

IF EVER there was a statement of intent regarding a potential Premier League title challenge, this was surely it. With the season barely a fortnight old, the Blues travelled to White Hart Lane to face Harry Redknapp's Tottenham who were also considered dark horses for a title tilt.

This was a venue the Blues had struggled at in recent years, losing six and drawing two of the previous eight visits so a point would have been an acceptable result before kick-off, but City came into this game brimming with confidence and looking to show just how far they had come under Roberto Mancini.

Samir Nasri was making his debut for City after joining from Arsenal so it was the first time he had played alongside David Silva, Sergio Aguero and Edin Dzeko – but within half an hour of this game starting, you would have thought they'd all played together for years.

Mancini, criticised in some quarters for being too cautious in his first full season, promised his team would be more attacking this season and he was as good as his word as City began the campaign with a sparkling 4-0 home win over Swansea and a thrilling 3-2 victory away to Bolton Wanderers.

Spurs had lost 3-0 to Manchester United – their only game so far – and went into this fixture in bottom place. They had a side packed with attacking players including Gareth Bale, Luka Modric, Rafael van der Vaart and Nico Kranjcar though new signing Emmanuel Adebayor, on a season-long loan from City, was not allowed to face his parent club.

Spurs started well and had Bale taken a fairly simple chance by his lofty standards when the score was still 0-0, this match may have gone down an entirely different path.

As it was, neither side found the net early on and it wasn't until the 34th minute that the deadlock was finally broken. Silva fed Nasri on the right and the Frenchman's whipped-in cross was expertly poked home by Dzeko in the six-yard box. It was the start of an unforgettable afternoon for the Bosnian.

Peter Crouch almost levelled for the hosts but his header hit the wrong side of the post and the Blues once again punished Spurs' profligacy moments later and it was the same combination who had opened the scoring for City that struck again when, a couple of minutes before the break, Nasri dug out a quality cross from the edge of the box and Dzeko cleverly rose to head in the opposite corner to what Brad Friedel was expecting and with 41 minutes gone the Blues were 2-0 up and on their way.

Nasri, formerly employed by Tottenham's arch-enemies Arsenal, was having a dream debut and his move to City was already looking a wise one.

Redknapp delivered a wake-up call to his players at the break, but there was to be no respite from the rampant Blues who quickly put the game to bed with two more goals before the game was an hour old.

First Yaya Toure burst into the penalty area and hit a low ball across the face of the Spurs six-yard box to give Dzeko the simplest of chances to complete his hat-trick and with the home fans and players still reeling, Aguero took on his marker down the left, darted past and shot as Friedel came to narrow the angle.

It was devastating, superb attacking football that a very good Tottenham side simply couldn't live with.

Trailing 4-0, Redknapp slumped on the bench looking stunned that his talented side were being systematically dismantled before his eyes. It wasn't so much Spurs were bad on the day, more the Blues were unplayable.

As the sunshine continued to beat down on White Hart Lane, City eased off the gas a little, safe in the knowledge that three points were in the bank.

Younes Kaboul pulled one back on 67 minutes from a corner, suggesting that there were still problems to be ironed out at the back, and for the next 20 minutes or so it was all Tottenham.

Hart was forced to make a couple of smart saves as the hosts attempted to regain a little pride and a second goal would have given the score a more palatable look for the home fans, but when van der Vaart limped off with ten minutes to go, it summed up the Lilywhites' miserable afternoon, though there was still a sting in the tail that would give the result a devastating look and perhaps more realistically represented the Blues' superiority on the day.

As the game ticked past the 90-minute mark, Dzeko picked up the ball around 40 yards out, played a short pass to Nasri who returned the ball into the Bosnian's path and fired an absolute beauty past Friedel for his fourth of the game to seal a 5-1 victory.

It had been breathtaking stuff from the Blues who moved up to second in the table, level on points with leaders United.

Spurs manager Redknapp promised his team would never suffer such humiliation during his reign again and he was right, though by the end of the campaign he had been relieved of his duties.

Perhaps the Spurs board had seen the gap between their team and City on the day and decided the club needed to move in a different direction. The travelling Blues didn't care either way. At last, they could travel back up the M1 dreaming of being crowned as champions.

55 v Hamburg 2-1

16 April 2009
UEFA Cup fourth round second leg
Attendance: 47,009

MANCHESTER CITY:	HAMBURG:
Given	Rost
Richards	Boateng
Onuoha	Gravgaard
Dunne	Mathijsen
Bridge	Jansen
Zabaleta (Fernandes 77)	Pitroipa
Kompany	Jarolim
Ireland	Aogo
Elano (Sturridge 84)	Trochowski (Petric 73)
Robinho	Guerrero
Caicedo	Olic

CITY HAD begun the quarter-final against Hamburg in the best possible way with a goal inside the first minute in the first leg in Germany. Things went downhill from there and the Blues returned home having been well-beaten 3-1 by the Bundesliga side, but there was still hope with the knowledge that a 2-0 win would take City into the semi-finals of a major European competition for the first time in 38 years.

The key was getting off to a good start and grabbing an early goal to heap pressure on Hamburg and hopefully disrupt their tactics for the evening.

What the Blues couldn't afford to do was concede an early goal – if that happened, the hosts would need four goals to win the tie and though only Premier League leaders Manchester United had scored more goals at home by that point, it was still a tall order.

The club invited supporters to bring their flags, scarves and anything else in order to create a hostile atmosphere and the teams walked out to a sell-out 47,000 crowd and an atmosphere the like of which the City of Manchester Stadium had never seen before.

The Robinho effect had worn thin as the season wore on with the lightweight Brazilian capable of complete apathy or brilliance depending on his mood – he had also failed to score for four months.

A virtuoso display from the £32.5m striker might just edge this tie, but it would be compatriot Elano, costing a fifth of that fee, who would be the star of the show with the kind of performance that only truly world-class midfielders were capable of.

With Shaun Wright-Phillips and Craig Bellamy ruled out through injury, Felipe Caicedo was given a rare start and Stephen Ireland was forced to play on the right wing – Mark Hughes's team had something of a lopsided look, but there was enough quality to get the job done.

The City fans were doing their bit and as the referee blew for the start of the game, it was time for the players to deliver.

Hamburg began brightly and looked as though they were keen to put the tie to bed with an early goal and with just two minutes on the clock Pitroipa nicked the ball away from Richard Dunne and was then felled in the box by a high challenge from the Irishman that looked like a blatant penalty, but perhaps the fact it happened so early saved Dunne and City.

Then Micah Richards had a great chance to open the scoring on eight minutes as he burst through with just the keeper to beat, but he lost his composure and fell as he was about to shoot and the ensuing scramble could have seen Elano score but the Germans managed to clear their lines.

Hamburg continued to look dangerous when they attacked and with just 12 minutes on the clock, the scenario the majority of the crowd had hoped wouldn't happen did happen as a combination of Pitroipa and Olic presented Guerrero with a chance that he swept past Shay Given to give the Germans the lead. City, now 4-1 down on aggregate, were in need of a minor miracle. Worse still, Hamburg were looking every bit as impressive as in their first-leg display – but the Blues were handed a lifeline just five minutes later as the ball struck Trochowski on the arm and the ref awarded a penalty. Elano made no mistake from the spot and suddenly there was belief in the stands once again.

It was end to end stuff but City couldn't quite build up the required head of steam with too many misplaced passes and Olic was giving Dunne, already on a yellow card, a torrid time every time Hamburg came forward.

With two minutes to go before the break, City almost took the lead as the brilliant Elano thumped a trademark free kick off the crossbar from 30 yards but a coat of paint meant the teams went off level at the break.

City came out pumped up and looking for an early goal – and this time they got it as Caicedo received Ireland's pass inside the box and, with a calm mind and quick feet, he dummied Jansen, who slipped, then touched it away from Boateng before passing the ball simply into the corner.

The fans went wild and the stadium was well and truly rocking but there was still plenty of hard work ahead, but 2-1 up, the aggregate was now just 4-3 in Hamburg's favour and with 40 minutes remaining, it seemed anything was possible.

Three minutes later Elano struck the woodwork again with another peach of a free kick that hit the post as the Blues cursed their luck, but with Elano in this mood, City were still in the hunt but when Caicedo missed an open goal a minute later, fans wondered whether it would be the Blues' night after all.

The Ecuadorian somehow managed to fire the ball over from four yards out with the keeper stranded – it was a devastating miss because, as good as City were, they had to make the most of this spell of almost total dominance.

Robinho was denied by keeper Rost just before the hour-mark and then Caicedo put the ball in the net after being put through by Ireland but he was marginally offside. It was frantic, thrilling stuff but City still needed a third goal.

Then, with 15 minutes remaining, Dunne was shown a red card after yet another clumsy foul – it had been coming but with the Blues down to ten men, it virtually ended all hope of a comeback but despite the reduced numbers, Richards and sub Danny Sturridge had great chances to score in the final minutes but fluffed their lines.

City went out of the competition, but they had gone down fighting.

v Blackburn Rovers 4-1

7 May 2000
First Division
Attendance: 29,913

MANCHESTER CITY:	BLACKBURN ROVERS:
Weaver	Kelly
Edghill	Grayson
Prior	Dailly
Whitley	Broomes
Jobson	McAteer
Horlock	Harkness
Pollock (Bishop 47)	Dunn
Tiatto	Jansen
Kennedy (Granville 80)	Flitcroft
Goater	Dunn
Taylor (Dickov 53)	Ward

A PITCH INVASION after a Friday evening 1-0 win over Birmingham City had been widely criticised by pundits and fans of other clubs because, despite going five points clear in second place, third-placed Ipswich Town still had two games to go.

One of those games was away to champions Charlton Athletic so with a superior goal difference, the Blues' fans felt their team was virtually home and hosed. The next day, Ipswich thrashed Charlton 3-1 at The Valley and suddenly the point needed away to a more than decent Blackburn Rovers became a much bigger obstacle.

City were unbeaten in ten games and had won six of those as they chased a club first – back-to-back promotions.

Blackburn gave the travelling City fans the maximum 6,000 ticket allocation but it was never going to satisfy the demand which was closer to 20,000. The end result was City fans were in every part of Ewood Park with perhaps 15,000 of the 28,000 crowd supporting the away team.

Bright, warm sunshine accompanied the mass exodus from Manchester but the blue army were in good spirits.

Rovers boss Graeme Souness had watched Charlton celebrate the title with a draw in the previous home game and he said he didn't want another promotion party in his own backyard.

He had already seen his team's own hopes of promotion die months ago after a poor run of form in the New Year that had seen just six wins in their previous 20 games though their home form had been solid all season – just three defeats in 22 matches.

The first half would turn into something of a freak 45 minutes as a nervy City were pressed back by Rovers who were clearly determined to deny the Blues automatic promotion and end their own campaign on a high.

They had underperformed for much of the season and a team including Garry Flitcroft, Matt Jansen, Damien Duff, David Dunn, Jason McAteer and Christian Dailly should not have been looking at a mid-table finish.

City hadn't created very much at all so when Broomes crashed a header against the crossbar from close range on 27 minutes, it should have been the wake-up call Joe Royle's side needed.

But instead, the warning went unheeded and a cross into the box on 43 minutes wasn't cleared and Jansen had time to control the ball and then volley in off the post to send the home fans crazy.

Suddenly everything had changed and a goal for Ipswich would put them in the box seat. It was an anxious half-time for everyone connected with the club – surely the Blues couldn't blow it?

Paul Dickov, the hero of Wembley just 12 months earlier, replaced Robert Taylor after the break but Rovers continued to look the more likely to score and on 58 minutes, a brilliant run by Duff set up Ward who turned inside Edghill before thumping a shot on to the inside of the post only to see the ball bounce back into Weaver's arms.

A coat of paint had denied the hosts going 2-0 up and if they had have scored, then nobody could have complained. In total, Rovers had by that point scored one goal and hit the woodwork three times. A minute later Jansen span and lashed a shot against the post as the Blues' luck somehow held out.

Ipswich had taken the lead in their game at Portman Road so as things stood, Ipswich occupied the runners-up spot and City had dropped to third. It wasn't quite panic stations, but it was getting very close to it.

Then, finally, the breakthrough came as Mark Kennedy broke down the left, checked, then played a short pass to Kevin Horlock whose delicious cross was stabbed home at the far post by – who else – Shaun Goater, who claimed his 29th of the season.

He had scored few more important than this, though, and there were celebrations all around Ewood Park and even on the hill overlooking the ground from where around 200 City fans were watching.

So Rovers had hit the post twice and City had scored – all in a three-minute spell. If fate ever played a hand in a football match, this was it and the gods were smiling on the Blues for once.

If confirmation was needed that there was divine intervention, it came seven minutes later when a long punt up front was absently headed back towards his own goal by Christian Dailly only to see his keeper almost directly behind him and the ball bouncing towards the empty net.

Yes, it was harsh on Rovers who should have been out of sight by that point but football can be both an incredible and cruel game.

Mark Kennedy made it 3-1 after 75 minutes with a clinical finish from inside the box and Dickov added a fourth six minutes later to once again score the last City goal of the season, though this time it merely sealed promotion rather than levelling the scores and forcing extra time in the play-off final.

There were perhaps 15,000 City fans who ran on to the pitch to celebrate what had been an amazing achievement by Royle's side at the final whistle.

A game that could easily have gone horribly wrong had ended with a 4-1 victory and the club that had slipped to mid-table in the third tier of English football – the lowest point in City's history – just 18 months before was now in the Premier League once again.

It was fairytale stuff but the dream would turn sour within 12 months as City were relegated from the top flight after just one season. The highs and lows of supporting this unique football club …

v Charlton Athletic 5-1

11 May 1985
Second Division

MANCHESTER CITY:	CHARLTON ATHLETIC:
Williams	Harmsworth
Lomax	Friar
May	Dowman
Clements	A. Kimble
Simpson	Gritt
Power	Aizlewood
Kinsey	Curbishley
Phillips	Harris
McNab	G. Kimble
Melrose	Flanagan
Tolmie	Lee

THE SCENARIO going into this game was simple – City had to win to gain promotion back to the top flight. Portsmouth were waiting in the wings for any slip-ups, but they knew the Blues would be in pole position, even though Billy McNeill's side had blown the chance to go up a week earlier with a 3-2 defeat at Notts County.

In fact, just two months prior, City had been on course for the title and sat six points clear, but the desperate need to get out of the division had seen a major wobble.

A disastrous run of three draws and three defeats meant McNeill's side had dropped 15 points in six games, fallen to third and now Pompey, Brighton and Blackburn Rovers were ready to pounce if results went their way.

Maine Road was packed to bursting point with more than 47,000 the official head count, but with the terraces burgeoning and every seat in the house taken, it's safe to assume the number was higher than that.

It proved that the Blues, who were in their second season in the Second Division, were still one of English football's biggest clubs, even if the performances on the pitch hadn't quite matched the might of the support who had turned out in their numbers for the past couple of years despite the slim pickings on offer from their team.

Charlton were the perfect opponents – they were safe from relegation and couldn't go up, instead floundering in the lower reaches of mid-table with nothing other than pride to play for.

Though Portsmouth must have hoped professional pride would be called into play, in truth the Blues would have to have a real off day for the Addicks to head back to London with anything.

City had lost their first choice central defensive partnership of Mick McCarthy and Nicky Reid through injury, but they still had more than enough quality to see the job through.

The roar that greeted the players on a searing hot Manchester afternoon was evidence enough of the expectations of the fans and the opening exchanges showed the City players were tense to say the least with a number of misplaced passes giving Charlton unexpected early encouragement.

The Blues needed a goal to settle their nerves and after just ten minutes, they got it. Paul Simpson picked up the ball on the left wing and headed towards the box and he looked up to see David Phillips arriving in the middle. Simpson's cross was inch-perfect and Phillips had the simplest of chances to beat Charlton's debutant teenage keeper Harmsworth.

A mini pitch invasion followed, much to the chagrin of manager Billy McNeill who waved the supporters off.

Moments later Jim Melrose broke clear but saw his low drive well saved by Harmsworth as City went for the jugular, but then Charlton broke and almost levelled when Steve Gritt rounded Alex Williams and only had Geoff Lomax to beat on the line, but the City defender somehow managed to block the ball and save the day.

The anxiety was palpable but the home crowd didn't have to wait long for the second goal.

Steve Kinsey won a corner on the left and Simpson's deep cross found full-back Andy May whose header looped up over the keeper and the defender on the line and into the back of the net, sending Maine Road wild. Just 15 minutes gone and 2-0 up, it was the best possible start for the Blues who now had one foot in the top flight.

Simpson went close to adding a third but there was no further scoring before the break.

One goal for the visitors could change the whole complexion of the match but any concerns were blown away in an explosive first 15 minutes after the break when City sealed their promotion.

First Paul Power whipped in a cross for Melrose to arch back and somehow power a magnificent header past a stationary Harmsworth to make it 3-0, then, just 60 seconds later, Simpson chased Neil McNab's high punt towards the Charlton box and as the keeper hesitated on the edge of the area, expecting the ball to have enough pace to make it to him, the City winger got a toe end in first which was enough to leave him with an open net to roll the ball into.

The fans went crazy as the realisation sunk in that the Blues were going up no matter what Portsmouth did in the other game.

But the Blues still hadn't finished and after Simpson again broke down the left and whipped in a cross, the ball was cleared to the edge of the box where Phillips arrived to drill home a powerful low drive into the bottom-right corner to make it 5-0. City had scored three goals in five unforgettable minutes.

Phillips had proved a particularly inspired signing by McNeill, costing just £65,000 from Plymouth Argyle, and his 12 goals from midfield had proved an integral part of the drive towards promotion.

Robert Lee pulled one back towards the end and Alan Curbishley hit the post as City lost their concentration but it didn't matter one jot – the final whistle went shortly after and Maine Road became a sea of people as fans poured on to the pitch to celebrate.

Just two years after the last-day relegation heartbreak against Luton Town at Maine Road, City were back in the big time and nobody was going to spoil their moment in the sun.

v Manchester United 2-1

8 April 2013
Premier League
Attendance: 75,498

MANCHESTER CITY:	MANCHESTER UNITED:
Hart	De Gea
Zabaleta	Rafael
Kompany	Evra
Clichy	Jones
Nastasic	Ferdinand
Milner	Giggs
Nasri (Aguero 71)	Carrick
Barry	Young (Kagawa 90)
Silva (Lescott 90)	Rooney (Hernandez 85)
Yaya Toure	Welbeck (Valencia 80)
Tevez (Garcia 90)	Van Persie

AT THE start of the season, a glance at the fixture list suggested this game could have a pivotal effect on the title race with City and United expected to go head to head once again.

After the previous season saw both Manchester clubs finish level on points at the top of the Premier League, there was no reason to believe that the 2012/13 campaign wouldn't be equally as close.

United had arguably stolen a march in the title race by winning the battle to sign Arsenal striker Robin van Persie and though Roberto Mancini complained he hadn't added the players he had wanted, only the departure of Nigel de Jong appeared to weaken his team.

The coming of one Dutchman and the departure of another would have a devastating effect in the coming months as the Blues stuttered into the new season with a definite title hangover and United started like a side still wounded from the dramatic way they lost the championship to City and were determined to refocus and get some payback.

Ultimately, it was all about experience and as the season wore on, a small gap at the top steadily grew until by the time this game came around, United had gone an insurmountable 15 points clear.

There was no way there was such a gap in quality between the teams, but the table didn't lie and the Reds' relentless winning streak and van Persie's goals meant that there could be no dramatic turnaround in fortunes this time – no eight-point lead thrown away like the previous season.

Arguably the most crucial result had been when United beat City 3-2 at the Etihad Stadium in the first meeting between the clubs. The Blues fought back from 2-0 down to peg the scores at 2-2 and then went looking for a winner only for van Persie to snatch victory with a last-minute free kick.

That was a crucial swing of six points and instead of the Blues going top of the table and preserving an unbeaten Premier League record, they found themselves six points adrift and never recovered.

Dismal defeats against Sunderland and Everton allowed United to increase the gap and with just eight games to go, the Reds were 15 points clear.

Though the runners-up spot wasn't guaranteed, there seemed little to motivate the City players other than local pride. Everyone knew things hadn't been right that season with injuries to key players a continual problem, but this was a chance to prove that despite the statistics and cavernous points gap, City were still the better team.

With that in mind and the thought of back to back wins at Old Trafford, the Blues bossed the early stages with crisp passing and movement that had the champions elect pinned back for much of the first half.

United were reduced to counter-attacks in their own backyard and the pace never let up in an exhilarating battle for local bragging rights.

All the first half lacked was a goal but within six minutes of the re-start, finally, with 52 minutes played, City broke the deadlock. A poor attempt at a back-heel by Ryan Giggs was stolen by Gareth Barry who played the ball to Samir Nasri. James Milner, outstanding all night, was well-placed and Nasri played a short pass to him and he fired a vicious low drive that clipped Phil Jones as it sped into the net.

He celebrated with a golf swing in front of the 3,000 delirious travelling fans reminiscent of Carlos Tevez's performance against Norwich 12 months earlier. The celebrations showed how much this game mattered to the players and the City fans and clearly there was a point to be proved.

But United struck back quickly and were level within seven minutes after Yaya Toure conceded a free kick in a dangerous position.

Van Persie swung in the ball from the right and Jones, just moments earlier cursing his part in the Blues' goal, saw his wayward header from two yards find the net via Vincent Kompany's back.

It was what the Reds had been doing all season – seemingly playing under par and then coming up with the goods at the vital moment, usually with van Persie, who City had desperately tried to sign, at the heart of everything.

The Blues, with an FA Cup semi-final against Chelsea to come and the hope of some silverware on the way – albeit not the trophy everyone had really wanted – continued to press and added a new dimension to the attack when substitute Sergio Aguero climbed off the bench on 71 minutes.

As City poured forward looking for a second, Yaya Toure clipped a pass to Aguero who had a sea of red shirts ahead of him on the edge of the box. With echoes of his title-winning goal against QPR a year before, he put his head down, turned on the after-burners and powered past four United players before firing a stunning shot past David de Gea for what would prove to be a goal worthy of winning any game.

City comfortably saw out the remaining 12 minutes of normal time plus the extras referee Mike Dean added on to record a satisfying 2-1 win.

The gap was reduced to 12 points and if nothing else, it delayed United's title celebrations by another couple of matches. It also proved that, despite the margin the Reds led the table with, there was little difference between the two Manchester giants. The win may have come too late, but pride was restored.

What nobody realised at the time was that this would be the last time Sir Alex Ferguson and Roberto Mancini took charge of a Manchester derby …

v Bolton Wanderers 1-0

23 April 1904
FA Cup Final, The Crystal Palace
Attendance: 61,374

MANCHESTER CITY:	BOLTON WANDERERS:
Hillman	Davies
McMahon	Brown
Burgess	Struthers
Frost	Clifford
Hynds	Greenhalgh
Ashworth	Freebairn
Meredith	Stokes
Livingstone	Marsh
Gillespie	Yenson
Turnbull	White
Booth	Taylor

FOR A side that had never progressed past the second round of the FA Cup in the first 12 attempts, the excitement at making it all the way to the 1904 final was close to fever pitch among City fans.

Record crowds packed into Hyde Road along the way and though Wembley Stadium didn't even exist, the thought of an exotic trip to London's Crystal Palace for the final ensured the cup run was the highlight of what proved to be the club's best season to date.

The Blues had been chasing a league and cup double with the title still a strong possibility going into the final weeks of the season. Ironically, the cup run probably scuppered the bid for the First Division championship with fixture congestion meaning six games in 15 days prior to the final itself.

City, managed by Tom Maley, had the legendary Billy Meredith among their number – a skilful winger with superb dribbling ability, he was a hero to thousands of football fans around the country and the first true superstar of English football. Forwards Sandy Turnbull and Billy Gillespie were also integral members of the City squad who had won the Second Division title the previous season and were continuing to improve as a team.

The cup campaign began with a home tie against Sunderland and an above-average crowd of 23,000 turned out at Hyde Road to see

Turnbull score twice and Gillespie add another in a 3-2 win over the Black Cats.

The draw for the second round pitted City with Woolwich Arsenal of the Second Division but the Londoners were no match for the Blues who won 2-0 with goals from Turnbull and Booth.

In an era when escapologist Houdini was the star of the day, the rights to *The Landlord Game* had been granted for production – better known as *Monopoly* today – and the New York subway opened for the first time, 1904 was an exciting, inventive time.

Meanwhile, City were now in the uncharted waters of the third round and were just two wins away from the final, but the record 30,022 crowd that packed into Hyde Road for the match against Middlesbrough were right to be apprehensive.

Boro had already inflicted a damaging 6-0 home win over City earlier in the campaign and also earned a 1-1 draw in the return fixture just a month before.

The crowd's hesitancy was well-placed as Boro ground out a hard-earned 0-0 draw to take City back to Teesside where the home fans had FA Cup fever, too.

Around 35,000 turned out for the third round replay but City banished the nightmare of the previous visit by turning in a superb display to win 3-1 courtesy of goals from Livingstone, Gillespie and Turnbull. The Blues were now just one game away from the final.

The semi-final was held at Everton's Goodison Park and attracted the biggest crowd City had ever played in front of with 53,000 paying to watch the Blues take on First Division leaders Sheffield Wednesday.

With the Owls closing in on their own league and cup double, City's trio of Meredith, Turnbull and Gillespie again delivered with a goal each when it mattered most as the Blues marched into the final with a convincing 3-1 victory. Surely there was no stopping Meredith and company?

Second Division Bolton had ensured it was an all-Lancashire final – a first for the competition – after beating Derby County 1-0 in the other semi. In the region of 30,000 fans travelled to London from the north-west on 23 April 1904 with many sleeping on train platforms at Euston and St Pancras having arrived the day before.

There was a typically convivial atmosphere between rival fans, as was the norm for the era, and the media attention was firmly focused on Meredith, who, of course, was more than happy to be in the spotlight.

The Blues had added incentive to win the cup having lost 1-0 to Sheffield Wednesday in the league after the semi-final triumph and also lost 3-1 to Newcastle meaning the title hopes were all but over.

City were in relaxed mood ahead of the big game and both sets of fans were determined to enjoy their day out.

With a crowd numbering 61,374 and tickets costing the equivalent of 25p, the teams ran out to contest the eagerly awaited 1904 FA Cup Final.

Dignitaries included Prime Minister Arthur Balfour and legendary cricketer W.G. Grace and if the majority of people had come to catch a glimpse of Meredith, they only had to wait 23 minutes for a piece of magic from the Welsh wizard who skipped past one challenge before driving into the box and planting the ball past Bolton keeper Dai Davies.

There was a slight suspicion of offside but no protestations were made by the Bolton players and there was even a one-man pitch invasion by a City fan who was quickly led away by police who, impressed by his passion, allowed him back on the terraces to continue watching the game!

Bolton enjoyed much of the ball thereafter but couldn't find a way past a resolute City defence with Blues full-back Herbert Burgess in particular outstanding throughout.

The team had one more league game to play at Everton before they travelled home with the FA Cup and thousands lined the streets of central Manchester to greet them. The love affair with the competition was well and truly underway.

v Portsmouth 2-1

28 April 1934
FA Cup Final (at Wembley)
Attendance: 93,258

MANCHESTER CITY:	PORTSMOUTH:
Frank Swift	Jock Gilfillan
Laurie Barnett	Alec Mackie
Bill Dale	Billy Smith
Matt Busby	Jimmy Nichol
Sam Cowan	Jimmy Allen
Jackie Bray	David Thackeray
Ernie Toseland	Fred Worrall
Bobby Marshall	Jack Smith
Alec Herd	Jack Weddle
Eric Brook	Jimmy Easson
Fred Tilson	Septimus Rutherford

CITY WERE still reeling from a second Wembley failure by the time they started on what would prove to be a memorable 1934 FA Cup trail. Thrashed 3-0 by Everton the previous April, skipper Sam Cowan promised he would lead his team back to Wembley the following season – and this time leave with the trophy rather than losers' medals.

The Blues had enjoyed some impressive FA Cup crowds the previous season, but nothing could have prepared the club for the record numbers that would see Maine Road packed to the rafters as cup fever gripped the city. Boss Wilf Wild was hoping it would be third time lucky for his talented team who had reached the semi-final in 1932 and gone all the way to the final tie in 1933.

The form around Christmas had been a concern to Wild whose team had recently lost 8-0 to Wolves, 4-1 to Derby County and 7-2 at home to West Brom – results that put a severe dent in the Blues' title hopes and often came out of the blue.

The quest for silverware began in earnest with a third round home game against six-time FA Cup winners Blackburn Rovers. Watched by 54,336 people – the largest crowd of the day – Eric Brook put City ahead before Rovers levelled. The Blues held firm and a brace from Ernie Toseland either side of the break secured a 3-1 win and a passage into the next round.

The fourth round draw appeared kinder, with a trip to struggling Division Two outfit Hull City who were battling against relegation. On paper, it looked like a walk in the park, but the cup has always been a great leveller.

City, however, appeared to have one foot in the fifth round by half-time with Alec Herd and Brook giving Wild's side a 2-0 lead, but the game was far from over and cheered on by a packed Boothferry Park, the Tigers finally roared and earned a shock 2-2 draw, their second courtesy of a Bill Dale own goal. Nonetheless, the City fans welcomed another opportunity to sample the magic of the FA Cup and almost 50,000 turned out on a damp, cool Wednesday afternoon to watch the Blues comprehensively dismantle the Humberside outfit 4-1.

Fred Tilson scored twice and Toseland and Bobby Marshall completed the rout to set up a mouth-watering battle of the roses between City and Sheffield Wednesday at Maine Road. The Owls had already won the league fixture 3-2 on the opening day of the campaign and fancied their chances against a City team who had lost back-to-back league games.

An astonishing crowd of 72,841 crammed into Maine Road but two goals from Herd was not enough to edge past Wednesday who held on for a 2-2 draw. The City fans, however, could not get enough of the competition and believed the tie was far from over.

Though it's difficult to put an exact number on the amount of travelling fans that journeyed across the Pennines for the replay, anywhere between 20,000 and upwards is perhaps an educated guess. Hillsborough was not ready for the Mancunian exodus and, tragically, there were many casualties including one man who was crushed and died on the terracing which simply could not cope with the swell of the massive crowd.

City were magnificent in a replay again played on Wednesday afternoon and triumphed 2-0 thanks to goals from Marshall and Tilson. Suddenly, Wembley was again within sight and two more victories would give Cowan the chance to ensure his promise was kept.

The Blues were paired with Stoke City in the quarter-final, who had a 19-year-old Stanley Matthews among their number and thousands of Potters fans travelled up to Maine Road for a game that would be talked about for decades as well as re-writing the history books.

It was a game, it seems, everyone wanted to see and a crowd of 84,569 somehow squeezed into the stadium – a record outside London that still stands almost 80 years on and Brook's superb goal settled a game the hosts deservedly won. Brook picked up the ball out on the left before curling a cross into the top corner of Roy John's net to send the crowd into raptures. Whether he'd meant it or not, it was a stunning goal and worthy of the occasion, though the dangers of such unrestricted numbers meant hundreds passed out in the crush and the ambulance crews were kept busy throughout.

City were in the semi-final and faced an Aston Villa side who had dumped out three-times winners Arsenal to reach the last four. A tight game was predicted but the Blues were by now unstoppable and Tilson was in magnificent form, firing four goals in a 6-1 thrashing of Villa at Huddersfield's Leeds Road. Herd and Toseland were also on target against Villa as City made it back-to-back Wembley appearances and though the previous two visits had ended in despair as Bolton triumphed 1-0 in 1926 and Everton 3-0 in '33, there was a feeling that this was the Blues' year.

Portsmouth had also made it to the final and were safe in mid-table while City were still chasing a top five finish – both teams had won their home league fixture so it was hard to predict who would return home with the trophy. Interestingly, Wembley officials noted the demand for meat pies went through the roof whenever a team from the north visited!

The game itself proved a nerve-shredding occasion for those who had made the journey from Manchester. Septimus Rutherford saw his shot squeeze through Frank Swift's fingers and into the net on 28 minutes to give Pompey the lead and with barely 15 remaining, City still trailed by that solitary strike.

But the Blues weren't finished. With 74 minutes gone and Portsmouth temporarily reduced to ten men through injury, Brook found Tilson and the City striker lashed home the equaliser to send half of Wembley's 93,258 crowd crazy. City pressed for a winner and on 88 minutes it came as Tilson fired home Herd's cross for a dramatic winner and ensure the Blues' second FA Cup success. The occasion proved too much for Swift who promptly fainted on the final whistle but the celebrations of an unforgettable day and a breathless cup campaign would live long in the memory.

And Sam Cowan had kept his promise…